our own state

MICHIGAN

history

and

geography

by

FERRIS E. LEWIS

Published by the

HILLSDALE EDUCATIONAL PUBLISHERS, INC.

Hillsdale, Michigan

39 North St. — Box 245   49242

T 15330

A Michigan History Textbook

ISBN 0-910726-25-6

Written by Ferris E. Lewis and revised by the staff of

Hillsdale Educational Publishers, Inc.

39 North Street

P.O. Box 245

Hillsdale, Michigan   49242

Made in Michigan

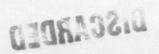

Table of Contents

The Idea of Geological Time Periods

Scientists have divided the time since they think the earth was formed into several periods. These groups have complicated names, but they are used often in this book.

These divisions were made because most scientists feel that special important events took place in each division. Events happened that changed the world from what it was before.

The Precambrian time is the first one of these divisions. During this time, the basic rock structure of the earth was formed. There are few fossils or other signs of life from this time. Many specialists believe the earth is about 4.5 billion years old. The radioactivity of certain elements help to prove this great age.

The Precambrian period lasted until 600 million years ago. There is no time of definite change, however. Near this time, life began to increase dramatically, and many fossils are found in rocks formed then.

Each of the time periods shown in the following chart refer to a certain time span which is written beside it.

The study of these time spans is important because it can tell you the age and something about the type of rock near the surface throughout Michigan.

The face of Michigan was scraped away by the glaciers leaving rocks formed during the different geological periods on the surface in certain places.

By looking at the map on page 6, you can see that the newest area of surface rock is in the center of the state. The older layers are beneath it. In other locations, near the Great Lakes, older rocks are on the surface. This gives you an idea when the surface rock in different parts of our state was formed.

SOME MAJOR GEOLOGIC TIME PERIODS AND THEIR NAMES

See the glossary for more information on each period and the map on page 6.

(time in millions of years ago)

4,500-600	Precambrian	400-340	Devonian
600-500	Cambrian	340-320	Mississippian
500-430	Ordovician	320-270	Pennsylvanian
430-400	Silurian		

Chapter 1

The General Geology and Geography of Michigan

Michigan — A State of Many Resources

Where people live and what they do to earn a living depends upon what natural resources are found in the area. If the soil is good and there is the right amount of sunshine and rainfall farm crops can be grown. Where there are minerals, mines or quarries are started and mining communities develop. If there are trees some men become lumbermen and trees are cut and sawmills are built. Where the necessary materials are to be had, manufacturing, such as the making of furniture, bricks or cement, may be started. If there are large lakes some men become fishermen while others become sailors and run large boats which carry, from one port to another, the products from the farmer's fields or the minerals from the mines or quarries. A forest area, where lakes and streams are found, may become a recreation area. People living there will make a living by caring for other people who come for their vacations. Sometimes cities develop where trade routes cross and goods are exchanged.

Because Michigan has many types of soil, several kinds of minerals, vast forests, many inland lakes and streams, and touches four of the five Great Lakes the people living in Michigan do several types of work to earn a living. In order for you to understand why there are so many different types of work you must learn how the resources we use today came to be here.

Michigan is the central part of a larger area known as the Michigan Basin that does include part of what is now Ohio, Indiana, Wisconsin, Minnesota, and Ontario, Canada. During the past few years people who study rock formations, called geologists, have learned much about the many changes that have taken place in the Michigan Basin since its early formation.

Long ago all the area of the Michigan Basin was under water several times as large bays of ancient oceans, or seas, spread inland. From the upland areas around the Michigan Basin rivers carried minerals and sediment into the ocean bays. This sediment was deposited on the ancient sea bottom. One of the minerals deposited was iron. Thus, layer upon layer of iron bearing material formed on the sea bottom in the area that is now the western part of Lake Superior.

After long ages this early sea bottom hardened and folded upward to form highlands, now called the Killarney Mountains, that ran from Wisconsin and Minnesota east across the Lake Superior area into Ontario. Part of this uplift ran through what is now the western part of the Upper Peninsula west of a line from Munising to Escanaba. Remains of this early uplift can now be easily seen in the Huron Mountains, the Keweenaw Peninsula and the Porcupine Mountains. As the sedimentary rock slowly buckled upward to form the

GEOLOGIC TIME PERIODS IN WHICH SURFACE
ROCKS WERE FORMED.
(time in millions of years ago)

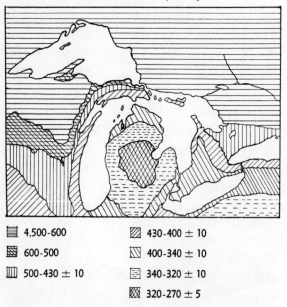

≣ 4,500-600   ▨ 430-400 ± 10

▧ 600-500   ◹ 400-340 ± 10

▥ 500-430 ± 10   ▧ 340-320 ± 10

▨ 320-270 ± 5

Killarney Mountains weak spots developed in some areas and hot lava, from deep in the earth, was forced upward to form volcanoes that spilled lava over much of the land. Also during this early period a large section of the area sank downward to form the present basin of Lake Superior. At that time deposits of pure copper formed in the area around the western end of Lake Superior. Some of the copper was deposited in the conduits of volcanoes while other deposits formed in cracks or between loose gravel.

As long periods of time passed the upland area slowly wore away. Streams carried pieces of rock and minerals from the highlands into the seas just as streams carry sediment to the ocean today. Thus, layers of sandstone, called Cambrian sandstone, formed on the bottom of other ancient seas that covered all the rest of the area now called Michigan. The northern rim of the Cambrian sandstone layers now outcrop along the south shore of Lake Superior. East of Munising the sandstone layers form what is known as the Pictured Rocks. Rivers spilling over the northern rims of the sandstone layers near Munising form some of Michigan's pretty waterfalls. Farther east Michigan's largest waterfalls, the Tahquamenon Falls, are

The Pictured Rocks on the south shore of Lake Superior east of Munising. This area has recently been made into a National Shore Park. (Mich. Dept. of Conservation Photo.)

formed as the water of the Tahquamenon River spills over the Cambrian sandstones. At Sault Ste. Marie, the rapids in the Saint Mary's River are formed by water flowing out of Lake Superior over the Cambrian sandstone. Like a huge saucer the Cambrian sandstone layers lie under the eastern part of the Upper Peninsula and the Lower Peninsula. Just west of Saginaw the bottom of the Cambrian sandstone layers lie some two and one half miles below the surface of the ground.

Later the rivers brought in less sand and large masses of limy sludge formed on the sea bottom in the Michigan Basin. This later changed to layers of limestone and dolomite. Slowly as ages passed the Michigan Basin became smaller and smaller as the sea filled with various sedimentary materials. Thus, the sedimentary rocks that underlie most of Michigan are like a group of smaller and smaller saucers placed one within the other. Each basin was smaller than the one before it because the sea became smaller and smaller as it filled in. The northern edges of some of these saucers swing in a large curve across the eastern Upper Peninsula. Some also come near the surface in the Detroit area.

LITTLE NIAGARA—Most famous of Michigan's more than 150 waterfalls, of course, is Tahquamenon Falls near Newberry. Hundreds of thousands of travelers pause each year to watch the copper-colored water slam over the 48-foot drop and boil on down toward Lake Superior. Tourists can drive within 300 feet of the falls and there are eating facilities nearby. (Mich. Tourist Council Photo.)

Geologists have divided these early periods according to the remains of life that are now found in these sedimentary layers. One of these early periods is called the Silurian Period. During this time thick layers of limestone and salt were deposited on the floor of the ancient sea. So large were the salt layers of this period, that underlie most of the lower Peninsula, that they run under Lake Huron and Lake Erie and go all the way to New York state. It is from these Silurian salt layers that rock salt is now mined at Detroit. The shaft of this salt mine reaches the salt bed at a depth of 1135 feet.

During the period following the Silurian Period, which geologists call the Devonian Period, more layers of limestone were deposited in the ancient seas. At these places limestone is quarried and used for making cement and smelting iron ore. Many kinds of fish and other sea plants and animals lived in the Silurian and Devonian seas. The casts of these are found in the limestone.

This map shows the general elevation in the state. The darker the area the higher it is. Each section shows a change of 300-400 feet. (You will notice that the upper peninsula is not in the right position on this map.)

By the time of the Pennsylvanian Period most of Michigan had risen above water. Only a small area, located in the central part of the Lower Peninsula, remained under water. Here a shallow swamp covered the area. The air was moist and warm and plant life grew well. The remains of this plant life, that once grew in this swamp, later changed to a bed of coal that lies under the central part of the Lower Peninsula.

Later the weather grew colder and the glacial age came on. Huge masses of ice formed near Hudson's Bay and under great pressure pushed outward in all directions. Down from Canada these huge masses moved. Sometimes they advanced forward only a few inches a year. Four times large masses, hundreds of feet in thickness and weighing countless tons, pushed down from Canada to as far south as the Ohio and Missouri rivers which were formed by the melt water on the southern side of the glaciers.

Some of the surface soil, that had formed in Canada during the ages before, was frozen fast to the bottom of the ice mass and carried southward as the ice moved slowly outward. That is why the soil, above the limestone layers, that now covers most of Michigan is called transplanted soil, for it was carried here from Canada by the glaciers. Thus, the soil of Michigan is different from the rocks upon which it lies.

The rocky tops of the Killarney Mountains pushed the ice masses upward as the glaciers passed over them but much of the tops of the mountains were carried away. When the glacial age came to an end there then lay close to the surface in this old mountainous area in the western part of the Upper Peninsula two of Michigan's valuable resources, iron and copper.

As the climate grew warmer again, the southern front of the ice masses melted farther and farther back to the north. As the ice slowly melted, and ran away as melt water, the changes that the glaciers had made, during long periods of time, could be seen. Much of the Killarney Mountains had been scraped off and carried away. The basins of the four lower Great Lakes had been gouged out of the limestone layers. Many smaller depressions, in the glacial till, became inland lakes. Huge ridges of glacial till, called moraines or hills, ran across the land. As time passed, these ridges became lower as newly forming rivers carried the glacial till into the lakes and valleys. Slowly soil formed and plants began to grow in the newly forming soil. Fish came into the lakes by way of the streams. Later trees covered most of the land. With plants and trees to feed on animals came to live in the forests. Because of the fish to catch and game to hunt men followed the animals into the forest land. Who these first hunters were we do not know but many artifacts, found by archeologists, tell us a few things about how these early hunters in Michigan lived.

The land area of Michigan is formed by two large peninsulas and several islands. The two peninsulas are known as the Lower Peninsula and the Upper Peninsula. They are separated from each other by the Straits of Mackinac. Some of the larger and better known of Michigan's islands are Bois Blanc Island and Mackinac Island in the Straits of Mackinac; Beaver Island in Lake Michigan; and Grand Island and Isle Royale in Lake Superior. Michigan has a land area of 57,980 square miles. It is one of the largest of the states east of the Mississippi River.

Most of the land surface of Michigan is level or gently rolling glacial till. The highest part of the Lower Peninsula is the area roughly bounded by Cadillac, Gaylord, and West Branch. This section is known as the "High Plains" area. Oakland County and Hillsdale County have hills reaching up to 1,200 feet above sea level. The eastern part of the Upper Peninsula is level or gently rolling land but in the western part in Marquette, Iron, Baraga and Gogebic counties the land pushes upward to over 1,600 feet. The highest point in the state, 1,978 feet, is in the Huron Mountains in the northeastern part of Baraga County.

Michigan touches the states of Ohio and Indiana on its south side, Wisconsin on its western side and the Province of Ontario, Canada, on its northern and eastern side. Michigan touches four of the five Great Lakes: Lake Erie, Lake Huron, Lake Michigan and Lake Superior. It also touches Lake St. Clair. These lakes and Lake Ontario form the largest group of fresh water lakes in the world. Because of this Michigan has a shoreline of about 3,251 miles. These lakes and some eleven thousand inland lakes, along with several pretty streams that flow through farm and forest lands, make Michigan one of the leading resort and vacation states in the United States.

Michigan's ten largest inland lakes in order of size are Houghton, Torch, Charlevoix, Burt, Mullet, Gogebic, Manistique, Black, Crystal and Higgins. Three large rivers separate Michigan from Canada, the St. Mary's, the St. Clair and the Detroit. Some of the largest and best known rivers in Michigan are the Huron, Saginaw, Au Sable, Manistee, Grand, Muskegon, Kalamazoo and the St. Joseph in the Lower Peninsula and the Tahquamenon, Menominee, and Manistique in the Upper Peninsula.

Checking Your Reading.

1. What two peninsulas make up most of Michigan's land area?
2. Michigan's highest point is in what county?
3. Which of the Great Lakes does Michigan touch? Point them out on a map.
4. What states does Michigan touch? Point them out on a map.
5. What Canadian province borders Michigan?
6. Where is the High Plains area located?

Map Work.

1. Look at a copy of the **Atlas of Michigan** edited by Sommers. There should be one in your school library. (It was developed by Michigan State University and is available from Hillsdale Educational Publishers and others.) Study pages 22-23 to get a better idea of the relief of the land. Page 26 is helpful too; it is an elevation map. To learn more about the development of glaciers see pages 26-29.

2. On a large map of the United States, or North America, be able to locate: the states of Michigan, Indiana, Ohio and Wisconsin.

3. On a map of Michigan be able to point out the following: Upper Peninsula, Lower Peninsula, Straits of Mackinac, Detroit River, Lake St. Clair, St. Clair River, St. Mary's River, Saginaw River, St. Joseph River, Grand River, Muskegon River, Manistee River, Au Sable River, Manistique River, Menominee River and the Tahquamenon River.

4. Be able to locate Michigan's ten largest lakes on your map.

5. Find the following on your map of Michigan: Keweenaw Bay, Whitefish Bay, Grand Traverse Bay, Little Traverse Bay, Thunder Bay and Saginaw.

6. On the outline map of Michigan print in the names Upper Peninsula, Lower Peninsula, Lake Superior, Lake Michigan, Lake Huron and Lake Erie. Put a star in the county that has the highest point in the state.

7. If you have trouble understanding the saucer shaped arrangement of rock layers under Michigan see the drawing on page 27 of **Geology of Michigan** by Dorr and Eschman. If you are interested in learning more about carbon-14 dating read pages 18-22 in this same book.

8. Compare the length of coastline in Michigan to that of the Atlantic coast (use an almanac to find that information).

To Help You Understand.

Look in a dictionary for the meaning of the following words; bay, peninsula, strait, island, surface, boundary, fossil and sediment.

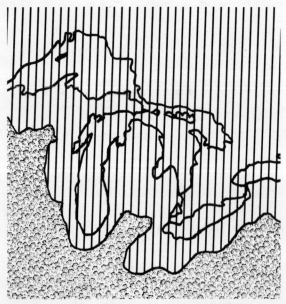

The position of the last glacier covering the Michigan area 14,800 years ago. The Great Lakes were formed by the glacier's melting.

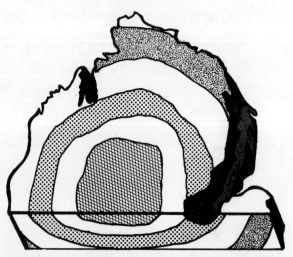

This is a piece of Michigan cut in two to show the kinds of rock layers beneath the lower peninsula. They are like several bowls set inside each other.

MAJOR RIVERS AND INLAND LAKES OF MICHIGAN
(Notice that several different rivers have the same name.
Pine and Black are used often.)

UPPER PENINSULA RIVERS
(From left to right)

1. BLACK	9. STURGEON
2. PRESQUE ISLE	10. INDIAN
3. ONTONAGON	11. MANISTIQUE
4. SILVER	12. TWO HEARTED
5. FORD	13. PINE
6. ESCANABA	T. TAHQUAMENON
7. RAPID	14. BIG MUNUSCONG
8. WHITEFISH	

LOWER PENINSULA RIVERS
(Starting from the left)

15. DOWAGIAC	34. PINE
16. ST. JOSEPH	35. AU SABLE
17. PAW PAW	36. AuGRES
18. BLACK	37. RIFLE
19. KALAMAZOO	38. TITTABAWASSEE
20. RABBIT	39. CHIPPEWA
21. GRAND	40. SAGINAW
22. THORNAPPLE	41. SHIAWASSEE
23. MAPLE	42. CASS
24. MUSKEGON	43. FLINT
25. WHITE	44. BLACK
26. PERE MARQUETTE	45. MILL CREEK
27. LITTLE MANISTEE	46. CLINTON
28. MANISTEE	47. ROUGE
29. BETSIE	48. HURON
30. BOARDMAN	49. RAISIN
31. PIGEON	
32. BLACK	
33. THUNDER BAY	

11

Chapter 2

The Indians in Michigan

How the Indians Lived

When the Frenchmen came to Michigan they found Indians living in the area. They had been here for thousands of years, but scientists do not believe they always lived here. No one knows exactly when they arrived. They traveled here from other areas. Their ancestors probably first arrived in the United States long ago from Asia. The tribes living here belonged to a large group of Indians we now call Algonquin. The Sauk Indians were living in the area around Saginaw Bay. Later they moved to Wisconsin. The Chippewa lived in the Upper Peninsula and the upper part of the Lower Peninsula. The Miami lived in southwestern Michigan along the St. Joseph River. From there they moved to northern Ohio. The Potawatomi lived in the area around Menominee. Later they moved to southwestern Michigan and northern Indiana and Illinois. When the Potawatomi moved to southern Michigan the Menominee moved to the area around Green Bay. The Ottawa originally lived along the Ottawa River, in Canada, but were driven out by the Iroquois and came to live in the western part of the Lower Peninsula west and north of Petoskey. No tribe of Indians lived in a large area of northcentral Lower Peninsula.

The Indians were still living in what is called the late stone age because they were using tools that they made from stone; such as, arrowheads, barbed axes, spearpoints, awls, tomahawks, and scraping knives. Most of these stone tools were made of flint from Ohio, if it could be secured by capture or trade, or from a flint-like material called chert that could be found near present day Norwood, or on the islands in Saginaw Bay. These stone implements were fashioned by striking the flint, or chert, a blow thus causing the unwanted material to flake away leaving the object being made to have a sharp cutting edge.

The Indians in this area lived in easily moved homes, that were called wigwams, made from small trees and bark or skins. First, small tree trunks were set upright in a small circle about twelve or fourteen feet in diameter. The upper part of the little trees were then bent inward to form a circle of arches to support the roof or top of the wigwam. A few trees were then fastened horizontally to these upright trees. Where the trees passed each other the Indians tied them together with strips of bark cut from the inner bark of trees. When the bark shrank and dried it formed a firm connection. Onto this

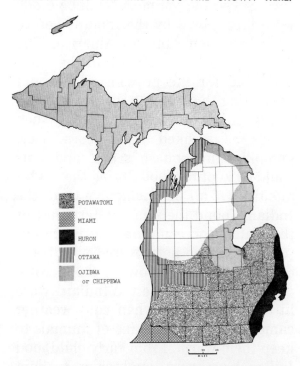

POTAWATOMI

MIAMI

HURON

OTTAWA

OJIBWA
or CHIPPEWA

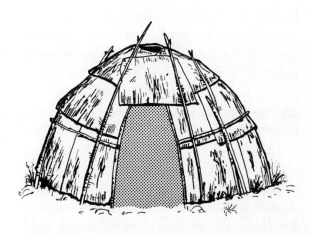

The Indians called such a building a wognanegon. In bark chapels the early missionaries held religious services.

dome shaped framework the Indians then fastened bark, or skins, to keep out the rain, snow and wind. Such a dwelling looked much like a large bowl placed upside down. On the ground inside the wigwam the Indians placed woven reed mats or animal skins. During the cold weather a small fire, in the center on the earthen floor, gave a little warmth to the inside of the wigwam. The smoke from the fire went out through a hole in the top. For firewood the Indians gathered fallen branches that they found on the forest floor.

The Indians depended mainly on hunting and fishing to furnish their food. Much of the Indian men's time was spent in securing fish and game. Fish were the main item of food for the Indians and usually they lived in areas where fish could be caught. Fish were plentiful in the streams, inland

lakes, and in the Great Lakes. These the Indians speared, netted, or caught on hooks made from bones or sometimes a small piece of copper. Ducks and geese were hunted by the Indians. The eggs of these birds were found and eaten during the nesting season.

The dense forest cover in most of Michigan shaded the ground and kept grasses and other small plants from growing. This lack of food for large animals meant that only a few deer, bear, elk and buffalo lived in most of the state. The largest number was found in the southwestern part of the state where small plains areas, known as oak openings, were found. In these areas, where grass grew, the larger animals could feed.

Small animals, such as, muskrats, beavers, rabbits, squirrels, and raccoons lived in the swamps and along the edge of the lakes and streams where the sunshine, necessary for plant growth, could reach the ground. Sometimes one of the larger animals was killed for food but the Indians depended on the smaller animals for their food. These they snared, caught in deadfalls, or killed by means of bow and arrow. Before the

French fur traders came into the Great Lakes area to trade with the Indians for animal furs the Indians killed only as much game as they needed for food. Animal skins were of little value and unless the furs were needed for clothing they were thrown away.

In the forests the Indians gathered, in their season, nuts, berries, and some plants, such as the jack-in-the-pulpit. These were eaten when ripe or stored for later winter use. In some areas wild rice was gathered. The Indian women would push a canoe into a marshy area where the wild rice grew. Then bending the stalks over the edge of the canoe they would strike the rice stalks with a stick thus knocking the rice into the canoe.

Although the Indians ate mostly small game and fish they did grow some crops and were Michigan's first farmers. But raising large crops was difficult for the Indians. Much of the area along the lakes and streams, where they made their camps, was poor soil. Because of their dependence on hunting and fishing, they seldom stayed long in any one place. Moreover, they did not have good tools that could be used in clearing the trees from the land. They had no shovels with which to spade the ground and only crude hoes, made from the shoulder blade of an animal or shell with which to cultivate the plants. In order to get a place to plant their crops they sometimes girdled trees and thus killed them. This let more sunlight reach the ground. On open prairies, or among the girdled trees the Indians planted such seeds as could be planted by pushing a stick into the ground to make a hole into which the seeds were planted. Thus, they grew such plants as beans, squash, pumpkins, tobacco and corn. Several of our most common foods were first grown by the Indians before the white men came to America. The Indian women did almost all the work in caring for the growing plants and harvesting the crop. As the Indians had few ways for preserving food only such things as smoked meat, corn, rice, pumpkin and squash seeds, and nuts could be kept for food during the winter months. Of all of Michigan's land, the Indians found the southwestern part of the state, where natural oak openings provided space not covered with trees, the best area for growing their crops.

In the summertime the Indians wore little clothing but when cold weather came they used the skins of animals to keep them warm. From early childhood Indian boys were taught how to hunt and fish and to know the secrets of the forest land in which they made their home. For hunting, and in battle against their foes, Indian men used bows and arrows and spears. The Indian girls and women did nearly all the work, such as, dragging home the game that the men had killed, preparing it to eat, gathering the firewood, tanning the deer skins for clothing, caring for their little gardens, and raising the children, while the men hunted and fished or went to war. Indian women also made baskets to keep their things in. These were made from strips of wood and sometimes the wood was colored with dyes made from nuts, bark, or roots. Some baskets were made of birch bark and decorated with colored porcupine quills.

During the summer the Indians gathered in larger groups at Sault Ste. Marie and Cross Village where fish were plentiful. When fall came the Indians left

Indian baskets

these summer camping grounds and separated into smaller groups. Usually these groups were a single family or two. Each family went to a winter hunting ground where there would be game enough in the area to feed a few people. The Ottawa from the Cross Village area usually went south to the Grand River Valley for the winter season. The winters were long and often very cold and sometimes the snow lay deep on the ground. Then it was difficult for the men to secure enough food. If this happened, the Indians often died from the cold and lack of food.

Catching maple sap to make maple syrup. Each of the buckets is emptied every day or two. The sap is then boiled to get out the water. It takes about forty gallons of sap to make one gallon of syrup.

When spring came, the Indian women caught the sweet sap of the maple trees in small birch bark cups. This sap they

boiled down to make maple syrup and maple sugar. The sap was placed in a large birch bark container and then stones were placed on the bottom on the inside. Onto these stones other hot stones were dropped to make the sap boil. After the Frenchmen came, with goods from Europe to trade for furs, the Indians used iron kettles for cooking and making maple sugar. Maple sugar, maple syrup, and now and then wild honey from a bee's nest were the only sweets the Indians knew.

There were no roads, in this forest land, such as there are in Michigan today. Some narrow trails, usually paths that had been made by large animals, led through the forest and swamps but these trails were seldom used by the Indians for traveling for any long distance. In the winter, when deep snow lay in the forest, the Indians used snowshoes to travel across the land or when hunting for game. The snowshoes kept them from sinking into the deep snow and made walking less tiresome. But most of their traveling was done during the warm weather and then the lakes and streams became the Indian's highways. Over these they paddled their bark canoes.

The canoe and the snowshoe were developed by the Indians for traveling in their native woodland. Both had been shaped into their useful state over many centuries, for an Indian canoe and the snowshoe were well adapted to traveling in the Great Lakes woodland area. A snowshoe was made by bending a piece of wood into a long narrow loop and then lacing it back and forth with strips of animal hide. The canoe was in fact an elongated birch bark basket that was used for carrying a group of people and their household or war supplies.

In making an Indian canoe no nails, or any other metal, were used. All the materials in its construction came from the forests of the Indian's homeland. To make a canoe the Indians first formed a wooden framework, about twenty feet long, of white cedar sticks. This cedar framework was fastened together with withes or strips of hide. It was about five feet wide in the center and gradually narrowed until the sides came together at each end. Sometimes, the bark of a single birch tree was large enough to cover the entire cedar framework of a canoe. At other times several pieces of bark were sewed together by using the fine root of a coniferous tree. The root of the red spruce was best if it could be found. When the bark had been fastened to the frame, by sewing and binding, the open places where the bark had been sewed together were ready for gumming to keep the water out. With the aid of a torch to melt the gum, from pine trees, the seams in the bark were made watertight. While in use canoes often had to be gummed every day to keep them from leaking. In some areas, where there were few birch trees, elm bark was often used in place of birch bark. Canoes were made higher at both ends so that they could better take the waves on the lakes. Usually each Indian tribe had its own shape for these canoe ends and one could tell to which tribe the canoe belonged.

In these light craft the Indians paddled, or polled, up and down the rivers, across the inland lakes, and along the shore of the Great Lakes. When they came to a shallow place in a river, a rapids, or a waterfall, it was necessary to carry the canoe and supplies along a path around the obstacle. Such a carrying place was called a portage. Hundreds of these portage paths beside the rivers, or going from one river to another, were scattered throughout the forest land. These portages were ages old before the Indians showed them to the early French missionaries and fur traders as they came into the Indian's homeland. Many of these portage paths are still used by travelers in Canada, north of Lake Superior, even today.

Checking Your Reading

1. What were the homes of the Michigan Indians like? Describe one.

2. To what large group of Indians did the tribes living in Michigan belong.

3. Name some of the Indian tribes that lived in Michigan. Where did each tribe live?

4. What do we mean by the late stone age? What kind of stone was used for making arrowheads and tools? Where was it found?

5. How did the Indians get most of their food? What were some of the crops that the Indians grew? Why didn't the Indians raise more crops?

6. Explain why large animals were seldom found in the forest areas.

7. Who did most of the work in an Indian village?

8. What two means of travel did we get from the Indians?

9. How were Indian canoes made?

Some Things To Do

1. Find in your library material telling about the Indians who once lived in Michigan.

2. If you have any arrowheads, or other Indian artifacts, bring them to school and show them to the class.

3. If there is a museum in your area that has material on Indians go and look at the display.

4. What Indians lived in your area? What can you find out about them?

Map Work

1. Many cities, rivers and counties in Michigan have Indian names. Shiawassee, Ishpeming, Pontiac and Owosso are some examples. Make a list of 10 Indian names found on the maps on pages 34 and 35. To be certain they are Indian names, read Virgil Vogel's book **Indian Names in Michigan.** (1986)

2. On an outline map of Michigan show where the tribes lived during the mid 1700's.

Michigan Indians Today

When people from Europe began coming to America, to settle and trade, the customs of both the Europeans and Indians began to change. The Indians found some European trade goods useful to them. Guns replaced bows and arrows; woolen blankets were used in place of furs for warmth; the flint arrowhead gave way to iron arrowheads. Axes, needles, beads, and other trading goods also changed the Indian way of life. From the Indians the Europeans adopted the canoe and snowshoe and hundreds of words common to our culture today, such as: toboggan, moccasins, chipmunk, and moose. Some of our most common foods like squash and corn are of Indian origin. Each culture has enriched the other.

The struggle for more and more furs did much to change tribal locations and set one tribe against another. In the colonial wars between the French and English both sides sought the aid of their Indian allies. Many Indians lost their lives in the European struggle for land and the fur trade. European diseases, before unknown to the Indians, like smallpox, further reduced the size and strength of the Indian population.

As the American settlements spread westward the Indians were forced to give up their land to the incoming settlers. In treaty after treaty more and more land was taken from the Indians. Usually the land was taken for a very small price. Many of the provisions of these treaties between the government and the Indians were soon forgotten once the settlers were moving into the land and the Indians were not strong enough to uphold their side of the treaty. Sometimes these treaties set aside small areas to be used by the Indians. These areas are generally called reservations. Often the land set aside was poor land for farming and too small to support people by hunting and fishing. Some Indians were taken farther west across the Mississippi River and forced to live on other Indian tribal lands. Some crossed into Canada. Their descendants now live on Walpole Island at the mouth of the St. Clair River. Only a few Indians were left in Michigan and these found themselves living in the midst of a different culture of which they were not really a part.

In 1834, just before Michigan became a state, the Congress of the United States set up a Bureau of Indian Affairs in the War Department. In 1849, the bureau became a branch of the Department of Interior. The purpose of this bureau was to administer the tribal lands and land held by individual Indians.

Indians were thought of as a people apart from the white man's culture and they were usually not allowed to vote. It was as late as 1924 when all Indians, living in the United States, were granted citizenship.

The Indians now living in Michigan are the descendants of the original tribes that once lived in the Great Lakes area. Some of them are of pure blood but many are descended from ancestors of various tribes. A large portion of the Indians now living have some European ancestors, especially French. Many white people, especially those descended from the early settlers, have some Indian blood in them. There are probably as many Indians in Michigan today as there were when the Frenchmen first came into the Great Lakes area.

Michigan's Indians are scattered all over the state. Most of them live in regular communities off reservations. Only a few of them are farmers or business men. Many of them work in factories or in the woods industries. Many villages, especially in the upper part of the state, have one or more Indian families living in them. Several Indians live at Peshawbeston on the Leelanau Peninsula. About 2,500 Indians live in the Traverse City-Petoskey-Cross Village area. At Harbor Springs there is an Indian school run by the Sisters of Notre-Dame. There is a Potawatomi settlement at Athens where the government assigned land to some Indians in 1844. Nahama, in Delta County, has a village of Chippewas. Some 4,000 Indians live in Detroit and its suburbs. They are scattered throughout the city but many of them live on Detroit's west side in the inner city. Other groups of Indians live in Michigan's other major cities.

Several federal government departments, such as, agriculture, housing, labor and health are concerned with the Indians and their problems. Besides these there are several state and national programs that provide aid to the Indians. Many of the Indian's problems are the result of their low income. What they need is more education for better paying positions but only Indians on reservations can qualify for government scholarships.

Michigan has four reservations, or restricted areas, that are under the jurisdiction of the Great Lakes Agency at Ashland, Wisconsin. This agency also has jurisdiction of the Indians living in Wisconsin.

The **Bay Mills Indian Community** is located west of Sault Ste. Marie. The property was purchased by the United States government in 1860 and is now held in trust for the Bay Mills Indians. Today 2,189 acres still remain as tribal land. 1,600 acres consist of forest land. Some of the Lake Superior frontage is on this Indian land. About 250 Indians now live in this community.

The **Hannahville Indian Community** is located west of Escanaba. This land was purchased by the United States government in 1913 and 1942. There are 3,408 acres of tribal land and 2,846 acres of second growth trees. About 150 Indians live here.

The **Keweenaw Bay Indian Community** was established in 1854 by a treaty between the United States government and the Chippewa Indians. There are two districts in this community located on the shores of Keweenaw Bay. The land area is 13,794 acres. 1,609 acres are tribal land, 8,124 acres are allotted land, and 4,016 acres are United States Title land. About 300 Indians live on this reservation.

The **Saginaw Chippewa Community** is located about three miles west of Mt. Pleasant. This reservation was established in 1815 and 1864 by treaties with the Indians. There are 1,223 acres of Indian land. 506 acres are tribal land and 717 acres are allotted land. About 350 Indians live here. Many are employed in Midland and Mt. Pleasant.

In general the standard of living on these reservations is much below average. Some Indians find work in the area but many families receive assistance from the state or county. Some men go from the reservations to the cities and find employment, save a little money, and then go back to the reservation where they feel less discrimination than when living in the urban areas.

Indians today face a conflict between tribal customs and those of the other Americans that surround them.

* INDIAN RESERVATIONS IN MICHIGAN *

Today all Indian children attend public schools and speak English. Only a few Indians can speak the native language fluently. However there has been a revival of Indian culture by the young people.

In 1964, a Commission on Indian Affairs was established in Michigan to deal with the social, economic, and cultural problems of the Indians. The Civil Rights Commission protects the rights of Indians against discrimination.

Can You Answer These Questions?

1. How did European trade goods change the Indian way of life?
2. How have the Indians benefited our culture?
3. What are some of the foods that you eat that were first raised by the Indians?
4. How was the land taken from the Indians?
5. What is a reservation?
6. What is the Bureau of Indian Affairs? What does it do?
7. When were the Indians given citizenship?
8. Where do the Indians live in Michigan?
9. How many Indian communities are there in Michigan?
10. What commissions now aid the Indians?

Map Work

Locate these places on a map of Michigan: Bay Mills, Sault Ste. Marie, Escanaba, Keweenaw Bay, L'Anse, Baraga, Ontonagon, Athens, Harbor Springs, Petoskey, Cross Village, and Walpole Island in Ontario, Canada.

An Indian boy gathers wild rice near the Hannaville Indian Settlement. (Michigan State Archives, History Division)

a. Isle Royal
b. Drummond Island
c. Mackinac Island
d. Bois Blanc Island
e. Beaver Island
f. Fox Islands
g. Manitou Islands
h. Grand Traverse Bay
i. Saginaw Bay
j. Lake St. Clair

The _Michigan History_ magazine has a history of one of Michigan's counties in each issue. They are appearing in alphabetical order and the first was in the May-June 1978 issue. Mason county is the first one featured in 1987.

Chapter 3

Michigan as Part of New France

The First White Men to Visit Our State

In 1608, Champlain and a group of Frenchmen made a settlement at Quebec, on the St. Lawrence River, in what is now Canada. These men came to trade with the Indians for the furs they took from the animals of the forest. Soon other men of the Jesuit Order of the Roman Catholic Church came to Quebec to bring the Christian religion to the Indians who lived in the area. Before many years had passed other settlements were also made along the river.

At first the nearby Indians brought their furs to the little settlements to trade for the goods of the Frenchmen but before long the local supply of furs became very scarce. The St. Lawrence River leading into the fur producing regions of North America enticed the fur traders and missionaries to go farther and farther west. One sought the furs that the Indians had to trade while the other wanted to live in the Indians' homeland and teach them about Christianity.

Unfortunately the Frenchmen living in New France, for that was what the area was called, allied themselves with Indian tribes who were enemies of the Iroquois, who lived in what is now New York State. These Indians controlled the upper St. Lawrence River and thus made it dangerous for Frenchmen to travel there.

Where Montreal now stands a river called the Ottawa joined the St. Lawrence River. This river led more directly to the west. So the Frenchmen turned their canoes up the Ottawa River into the land of the Ottawas, who were their friends. When they came to the little river now called the Mattawa they followed it westward through Lake Talon to its source in Trout Lake. All this way they had been paddling up stream. From Trout Lake they portaged over a divide to Lake Nipissing. From this lake the Frenchmen drifted down the French River to Georgian Bay. Thus, the Frenchmen, traders and missionaries, found the route into the Great Lakes area. By going south to the lower end of Georgian Bay they came to the homeland of their friends the Huron Indians, who lived between Lake Ontario and Georgian Bay in an area known as Huronia.

No one knows who the first Frenchman to venture on westward to what is now Michigan was, but it is believed that Brulé reached the area soon after 1620. He was one of the young men Champlain sent to live with the Indians to learn their language and about the geography of the country. In 1634, an

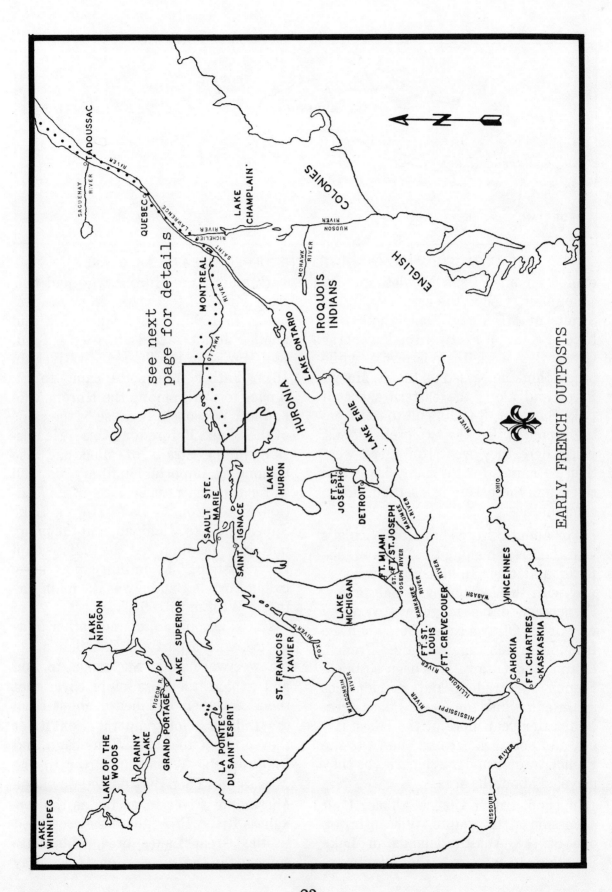

EARLY FRENCH OUTPOSTS

LAKE WINNIPEG

LAKE OF THE WOODS

RAINY LAKE

GRAND PORTAGE

PIGEON R.

LAKE NIPIGON

LAKE SUPERIOR

LA POINTE DU SAINT ESPRIT

ST. FRANCOIS XAVIER

SAULT STE. MARIE

SAINT IGNACE

LAKE MICHIGAN

FOX RIVER

WISCONSIN RIVER

FT. ST. JOSEPH

DETROIT

FT. MIAMI

FT. ST. JOSEPH

ST. JOSEPH RIVER

KANKAKEE RIVER

MAUMEE RIVER

FT. ST. LOUIS

FT. CREVECOUER

ILLINOIS RIVER

CAHOKIA

FT. CHARTRES

KASKASKIA

VINCENNES

WABASH

OHIO RIVER

MISSISSIPPI RIVER

MISSOURI RIVER

LAKE HURON

LAKE ERIE

HURONIA

LAKE ONTARIO

IROQUOIS INDIANS

MOHAWK RIVER

HUDSON RIVER

ENGLISH COLONIES

LAKE CHAMPLAIN

RICHELIEU RIVER

SAINT LAWRENCE RIVER

MONTREAL

OTTAWA RIVER

QUEBEC

SAGUENAY RIVER

TADOUSSAC

N

see next page for details

23

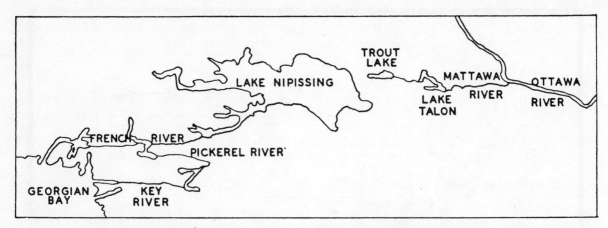

THE VOYAGEURS' HIGHWAY INTO THE UPPER GREAT LAKES AREA

explorer named Jean Nicolet, sent by Champlain, visited the area around the Straits of Mackinac. Some think that Nicolet went on westward as far as the Green Bay area, in Wisconsin, while others think he passed up the St. Mary's River and along the eastern shore of Lake Superior. It is difficult to tell from the accounts that the explorers left us, just where they went, for there were then no names for the many lakes and rivers and there were few settled Indian communities.

For about thirty years after Nicolet's visit the French along the St. Lawrence River and their Indian allies were at war with the Iroquois and only a few Frenchmen dared to go westward by way of the Ottawa River. But, when the Iroquois raids against the French, Huron, and Ottawa had been stopped, French fur traders and missionaries again came into the Great Lakes area. Year after year more of the lakes, rivers, and portages became known to the French traders and missionaries as they traveled about the area.

In 1666, Father Claude Allouez built a mission at La Pointe, Wisconsin, on one of the Apostle Islands in Lake Superior, to continue the missionary work among the Hurons who had fled from Huronia to escape from the Iroquois. In 1668, Father Marquette and another Jesuit started a mission at Sault Ste. Marie, on the St. Mary's River. In 1671, Father Marquette came to St. Ignace to work among the Hurons who had left Wisconsin because of the raids of the Sioux. Before long this little mission on the Straits of Mackinac also became an important military, as well as fur trading, post because of its location in relation to Lake Huron, Lake Superior, Lake Michigan, and the many portages leading to the Mississippi River system. The military post here, called Fort de Baude, was the main one in the West until 1697.

In 1673, Louis Joliet and Father Marquette, with a party of Frenchmen, set out westward from St. Ignace to find and explore the Mississippi River that the Frenchmen had heard about from the Indians. Going up the Fox River they crossed to Lake Winnebago and followed the Wisconsin River to the Mississippi. Then they floated down the Mississippi River to as far as the Arkansas River. From there they returned to the Great Lakes area. Marquette stopped at the mission on Green Bay

24

while Joliet went on to Quebec to report on their work.

The following fall Father Marquette began a journey to the Illinois country to work among the Illinois Indians he had visited while on his way down the Mississippi River the year before. But becoming ill on the way he found it necessary to spend the winter near where Chicago now stands. In the spring he and his party went on to the Illinois country. But being ill and unable to continue his work he promised to send another missionary and set out to return to his mission at St. Ignace. With two companions Father Marquette came northward along the eastern shore of Lake Michigan. He was unable to make the journey and died somewhere along the northern shore of the lake. The following year his remains were taken, by friendly Indians, to St. Ignace and buried beneath the mission chapel.

Father Allouez continued to do mission work for over twenty years. He was buried somewhere in the area of Niles.

Soon after the death of Father Marquette, another Frenchman, a fur trader and explorer named La Salle, became a leader in New France. La Salle built Fort Frontenac on Lake Ontario, where Kingston now stands. Instead of taking the furs in canoes along the Ottawa-Mattawa-French River route, La Salle wanted to build sailboats that would sail on the Great Lakes and carry cargoes of furs and trade goods. He had his men build one on Lake Ontario.

Then they carried the needed supplies, ropes, anchors, and sails across the Niagara portage and built a second sailboat on the shore of Lake Erie, just above Niagara Falls. It was named the Griffin. In the spring of 1679 the Griffin sailed westward across Lake Erie. Turning north the Griffin entered the Detroit River. Going up the St. Clair River it entered Lake Huron. After a stormy voyage on Lake Huron the little sailboat reached St. Ignace. From there La Salle and his men sailed on to Green Bay, Wisconsin. There the Griffin was loaded with furs that La Salle's men had bartered from the Indians during the previous winter. The Griffin then set sail on her return trip to the Niagara River but she was never seen again. The loss of the Griffin with her valuable cargo of furs was a great loss to La Salle and his plans for the development of New France. It happened like this:

After the Griffin left Green Bay, La Salle and his men made their way down Lake Michigan to the mouth of the St. Joseph River. Here they built a little fort and named it Fort Miami after the Miami Indians who were then living in the area of southwestern Michigan. Here they waited for the Griffin to return. When it did not come, La Salle and some of his men went on into the Illinois country where they spent the winter. The following spring La Salle and a few other men walked across lower Michigan on their way back to Quebec. This was the first group of Frenchmen to cross lower Michigan.

How Well Did You Read?

1. What was Champlain's settlement on the St. Lawrence River called?

2. What religious order did missionary work in New France?
3. By what route did the French fur traders and missionaries come to the Great Lakes? Tell why they came that way.
4. Which of the Great Lakes was discovered first? Why?
5. Who was Nicolet? Where did he go? Why is it difficult to know just where the early explorers went?
6. Who was Father Marquette? What did he do? Where was he later buried?
7. Who was Louis Joliet and what did he do?
8. By what route did Joliet and his party reach the Mississippi River?
9. Who was Father Allouez? Where was he buried?
10. Who was La Salle? Why did he want to build sailboats on the Great Lakes?
11. What was the Griffin? What became of her?
12. Where did La Salle build Fort Miami? What city is located there now? Find it on your map of Michigan.

Things to Do.

1. What can you find in the material in your library about the following Frenchmen: Marquette, Allouez, Brulé, Nicolet, Joliet, La Salle, and Frontenac? For the story of a woman in Michigan's early history, read "The Search for Madame Cadillac" in the magazine, **Chronicle**—Spring 1984.

2. Get a history of Canada from your library and read what it has to tell about the French settlement of New France and the early fur trade.

3. See what else you can find out about the kinds of food carried by the French traders and voyageurs.

Map Work

1. On a large map of North America, or Canada, point out the route that the Frenchmen took to reach the land of the Lakes. Put it in red on your outline map.

2. On the outline map print in the names of the following: Montreal, Quebec, Ottawa River, Mattawa River, Lake Nipissing, French River, Georgian Bay, St. Lawrence River, Lake Huron, Lake Superior, Lake Ontario, St. Mary's River, Sault Ste. Marie, St. Ignace, Niagara River, Mississippi River, Straits of Mackinac, Detroit River, and Green Bay.

3. Show the route Father Marquette took to go down the Mississippi.

The French Control Michigan

During the one hundred and fifty years that France claimed the Great Lakes region, animal furs were the major product of New France. Furs were in great demand in Europe at that time. Fur coats were worn to keep people warm. Then, too, much of the fur was used for making felt. The soft hair of the beaver, with its little barbs on the side, was sought after by European felt makers as it made the highest quality of felt.

The St. Joseph River at Niles. This was one of the main river routes in going from the Great Lakes to the Mississippi River system.

To get more and more furs, especially beaver pelts, the French fur traders went farther and farther west into new areas where animals were more plentiful. Using the Ottawa-Mattawa-French River route they entered the Great Lakes area. From there they went to Green Bay and then by way of the Fox and Wisconsin rivers to the Mississippi River. Others crossed at Chicago while others portaged from the St. Joseph River to the Illinois River. But the main trade route of the French fur traders went up the St. Mary's River to Lake Superior and then along its southern shore to where Duluth, Minnesota, now is located. From there they followed the shore of Lake Superior northeastward to Grand Portage near the mouth of the Pigeon River. From Grand Portage by means of lakes and rivers they went on into the colder lands of the north and west where the furs were the best because of the colder winters.

When the Frenchmen came to New France they found the Indians using canoes as a means of traveling and also carrying their household goods or war supplies. From the Indians the Frenchmen learned how to make canoes. Then with their better tools they made canoes that were both larger and stronger. During the warmer weather the Frenchmen used canoes as a means of traveling to and from the fur country of the west. Canoes also became the carriers of the furs and trade goods in the western fur trade.

The large canoes that were used in going between Montreal and Grand Portage, on Lake Superior, were called Montreal canoes or "canot du maitre." They were about twenty-five feet long, five feet wide in the center, and about four feet deep. These Montreal canoes could carry two or three tons of freight as well as the canoemen and their provisions. Smaller canoes, known as North canoes or "canot du nord" were used in going to and from Grand Portage to the fur trading areas farther west and north. The men who paddled the canoes were known as "voyageurs" meaning travelers. Illegal fur traders, men without permits from the king, were called "coureur de bois" which meant woods runners.

Packages of trade goods and bundles of fur usually weighed about ninety pounds each. Trade packages contained a variety of trade items so that a trader could supply the various needs of the Indians. Kegs of brandy were also brought west in the trading canoes. In

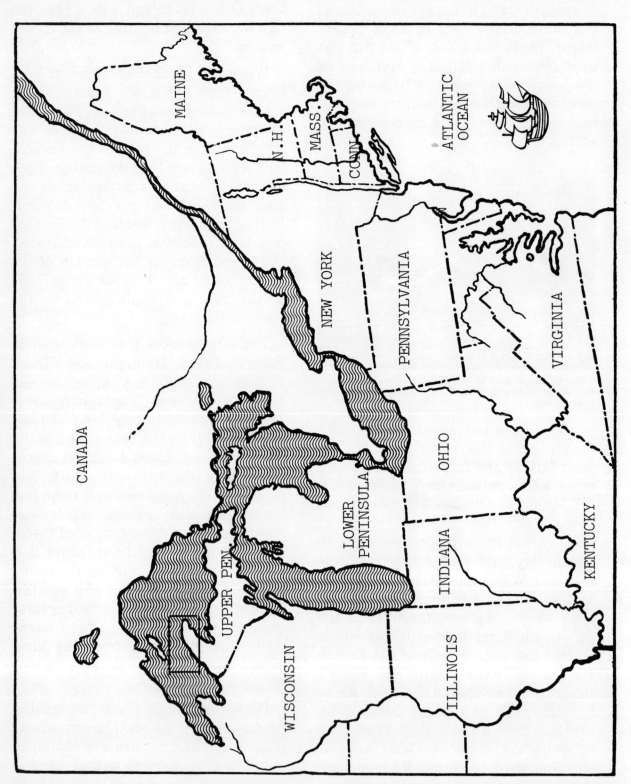

Northeast United States

ATLANTIC OCEAN

MAINE

N.H.

MASS.

CONN.

NEW YORK

PENNSYLVANIA

VIRGINIA

CANADA

OHIO

LOWER PENINSULA

UPPER PEN.

INDIANA

KENTUCKY

WISCONSIN

ILLINOIS

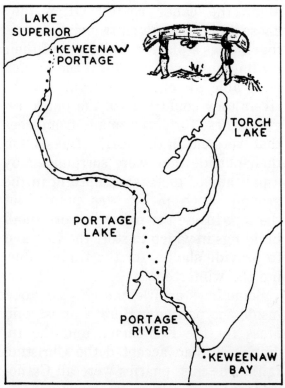

The Keweenaw Portage Route across the Keweenaw Peninsula.

loading, or unloading, these bundles and kegs had to be carried by the voyageurs between the shore to the canoes for the canoes were too frail to be drawn upon the beach. Usually two men held a canoe while it was being loaded and unloaded. At each portage it was necessary to carry all supplies, merchandise, or furs as well as the canoe around the obstacle. In going from Montreal to Grand Portage there were thirty-five portages. One of these portages was at Sault Ste. Marie, in Michigan. It was about a mile in length. Still another Michigan portage was at the southern end of the Keweenaw Peninsula. Instead of going all the way around the rocky Keweenaw Peninsula people going along the trade route used the Keweenaw Portage. From Keweenaw Bay they entered Portage Lake and followed it to its western end. From

there they portaged for about a mile to Lake Superior.

In making a portage each man usually carried two bundles of merchandise or furs and went at a trot along the portage path. Often several trips were made by each man before all the freight and supplies had been transported around the obstruction.

As the distance from Montreal to the trading areas grew longer and longer in the later years of the fur trade it was not possible, by canoe transportation, to go from Montreal to the distant trading posts, like on Lake Athabasca, and return to Montreal in a single summer season. So when spring came, voyageurs left Montreal with trade goods and the winterers left their posts in the far North, or West, with their canoes loaded with furs. Both groups set out for Grand Portage on Lake Superior. Here they met in midsummer and exchanged their loads of trade goods and furs. Then the voyageurs from Montreal returned to Montreal with the furs while the winterers hurried to get to their distant posts before the streams froze over in the fall and canoe travel would no longer be possible.

The French fur traders and their Indian friends traveled together for protection against the Iroquois who often waited along the trade route to capture the furs. Such parties went forty to fifty miles in a day. The distance traveled was spoken of in "smokes" or "pipes" and not in miles. This custom came from the practice of voyageurs resting every once in a while for a few minutes. During these rest periods the voyageurs lighted their pipes and smoked. Such rest periods were necessary as the canoemen usually paddled at the rate of forty strokes a minute with their short paddles. As the Frenchmen paddled their canoes they often sang the popular songs of the day. As they sang they kept time to their songs with their paddles.

France made little effort to settle the vast areas she claimed as New France that reached from Quebec to New Orleans and included all the St. Lawrence and Mississippi River systems as well as the lands north and west of Lake Superior. Most of the Frenchmen who came into the wilderness were soldiers, fur traders, or missionaries. The fur traders were welcomed by the Indians because they brought the Indians guns, powder, brandy, woolen blankets, iron arrowheads, tomahawks, copper and iron kettles, and other trade goods made either in France or along the St. Lawrence River in the French settlements. To get these things the Indians traded the furs they had gathered during the winter. The early fur traders usually lived with the Indians and often adopted many of the Indian ways of life. Some married Indian women.

To keep the fur trade from the English, in New York state, the French fur traders built forts at important places along the canoe routes. Often they chose a place at which two rivers came together as a place to build one of their trading posts, or forts, for if the French were able to control the traffic on the rivers they could control the entire region. These forts were made from trees that were cut in the nearby forests. On their outside they were surrounded by a palisade of pickets set upright in the ground. Each picket was pointed at the top. Inside the palisade were small buildings in which to store the furs and to provide shelter for the traders during the wintertime.

Sometimes a little church also stood inside the palisade. Here a priest said Mass for the Frenchmen and the Indians who had accepted the Christian faith. The missionaries were all Catholic then.

In order to strengthen their posts against unfriendly Indians the Frenchmen often encouraged friendly Indians to build their wigwams nearby. Then the Indians would bring their furs to the post, warn the Frenchmen if an enemy were coming, and aid in defending the post and settlement if it were attacked.

Checking Your Reading.

1. What was the major trade article sent from New France?
2. How were the furs that were sent to Europe used?
3. Why was the fur of the beaver the most wanted fur?
4. Why did the fur traders push farther and farther west?
5. By what routes did the French fur traders reach the Mississippi River?
6. How did the Frenchmen carry the trade goods and furs?
7. What were "voyageurs"? Coureur-de-bois?
8. Why did the Frenchmen want friendly Indians to live near their trading posts?

9. Where were the trading posts usually built? Why?

10. What were portages?

11. Where were the trade goods and furs exchanged in transit? Why?

12. How did the French voyageurs speak about distances traveled?

13. What two sizes of canoes were used in the fur trade? Can you tell why?

Things to Do and Talk About

1. Are there any places near your community that have French names? How did these places get their names? Use a French-English dictionary to see what some of the names mean.

2. Find French names on your map of Michigan.

3. Can you find any material in your library telling about the early fur trade in New France? Look at the book **Michigan Fur Trade** by Ida Johnson. It is an old book available in reprint form.

4. What animals did the Indians trap for their fur? How did they trap them?

5. Why are furs not so much in demand today?

6. Read "Michigan Wildlife Sketches" by Charles E. Schafer.

7. How are modern canoes different from the canoes used by the French fur traders?

French Forts and Settlements in Michigan

Little effort was made, during the years France claimed New France, by the mother country to send French settlers to the St. Lawrence or Mississippi River valleys. When France lost the area to England, in 1760, there were only about 80,000 people living in New France and they were scattered all the way from Quebec to the lower Mississippi area. After the first few years only Roman Catholics were allowed to come to New France. Most of the colonists lived along the St. Lawrence valley between Quebec and Montreal. That is why the Canadian Province of Quebec is French speaking and Roman Catholic today. Those who came westward were mostly fur traders, soldiers, and missionaries but a few farmers did start farms near some of the western posts.

In 1668, Father Marquette started a mission to the Chippewas at Sault Ste. Marie. This mission at the sault became Michigan's first settlement. But the mission here lasted only a few years. In 1671, Father Marquette started another mission at St. Ignace on the north shore of the Straits of Mackinac. Until 1697 this post was the main trading post in the area but it was abandoned when the king of France ordered all fur traders out of the West. In 1686, Duluth built a fort at the south end of Lake

Huron on the St. Clair River, where Port Huron now stands, in order to control the entrance into the fur areas by way of the Detroit and St. Clair rivers. Because of war with the Iroquois this post was soon abandoned.

Marker to Father Marquette at St. Ignace. (Mich. Tourist Council photo.)

About this time the Englishmen, from the Hudson River area, began coming into the lake region to trade with the Indians for their furs. In trading with the Indians the French used brandy. The English used rum and because of its cheapness they could give a larger quantity in exchange for furs than the French could give of brandy. Then, too, the English trade goods were of better quality than those made by the French in France and New France. Because of this, and the recalling of the French fur traders, in 1697, many Indians began to trade with the English fur traders. To stop this English fur

trade in the Great Lakes area permission was granted to Cadillac to build a post and settlement on the Detroit River.

Cadillac was one of the leaders of New France at that time and was well acquainted with the situation in the Great Lakes area for he had been commandant of the post at St. Ignace, when the soldiers and traders were ordered out of the West.

In June 1701, Cadillac and one hundred Frenchmen, in twenty-five canoes, set out from Montreal. Going by way of the Ottawa-Mattawa-French River route the party came to Georgian Bay. Coming down Lake Huron they entered the St. Clair River. Down this river and across Lake St. Clair the Frenchmen paddled their canoes.

From Lake St. Clair they went on down the Detroit River to Grosse Ile. Along the way the party carefully searched the river bank to find the best location for a post and settlement. After spending a night on Grosse Ile, they decided that the best place would be where downtown Detroit now stands. So Cadillac and his party returned up the river and chose the high river bank just west of the present foot of Woodward Ave.

The canoes were unloaded and everyone was soon busy felling trees to be used in building the palisade and the little buildings within. Thus, on July 24th, 1701, began the settlement that has since grown to be not only Michigan's largest city but also one of the largest cities in the United States.

About this same time another post, called Fort St. Joseph, was built on the St. Joseph River in southwestern Michigan near the place where the city of

Niles now stands. A few French farmers came to live at these two posts. Their little cabins stood in a line along the river bank and their farms were narrow, parallel strips of land that stretched back into the uncleared forest land. Only a few crops were grown as there was no market except such as could be sold to passing traders. There were a few Indian and black slaves, that did domestic work, in New France but slavery did not fit into the economic system of the fur trade.

Until 1710, Cadillac was in command of the little settlement on the Detroit River. The post was known as Fort Pontchartrain and the settlement was called Ville de troit, which means village of the straits. As time passed the ville was dropped and the settlement began to be called Detroit. All the buildings, except the farmers' cabins, that sat in a row along the river bank, were inside the stockade which enclosed an area about the size of two city blocks. When Cadillac was made governor of Louisiana the settlement declined but it still held on until its surrender to the English in 1760.

About 1715, the Straits of Mackinac again became the center of the French fur trade in the Great Lakes area. A little post, called Fort Michilimackinac, was built where Mackinaw City now stands. A replica of this fort has now been built and many people visit it each summer.

From the time the first crude stockades were built along the trade routes until 1760, the French were the masters of the land. For one hundred fifty years France claimed the area now known as Michigan. Though France held this area for all this time little was done to change it. If it were not for the many French names of places in Michigan that have come down to us, one would not know that France was once the master of a large part of North America.

In 1756, war developed between the English colonies and New France. It was called the French and Indian War in America and the Seven Years War in Europe. Michigan was too far west to play an important part in this colonial struggle but Frenchmen and Indians from Michigan did go east to take part in the battles fought there. Finally Quebec and Montreal were captured by the English forces and New France surrendered to the English. They had no choice because these cities control the St. Lawrence river (see page 23). When peace was made at Paris, in 1763, New France, except the islands of St. Pierre and Miquelon, became an English possession.

Reading Checks

1. At what two places did Father Marquette start missions?
2. What country wanted to enter the area and get furs?
3. Who was Cadillac? What route did he follow in coming to settle Detroit?
4. Why did the French want a post on the Detroit River?
5. Where did Duluth build a fort? Can you explain why he chose this place?
6. Name some of the articles that the Frenchmen used to trade with the Indians for their furs.

7. Which fur post was the most important one in this area during the time the French held the area? Why was this so?

8. How long did France control the area now called Michigan?

9. What name did Cadillac give to his little fort?

Some Things to Do

1. Check into your family background and see if you have any French or Indian relations. You could use old family Bibles or diaries which often have family information recorded in them.

2. Why didn't more French women come with the men to settle in Michigan?

3. Do some research and find out why the French and English were fighting each other so often in this period.

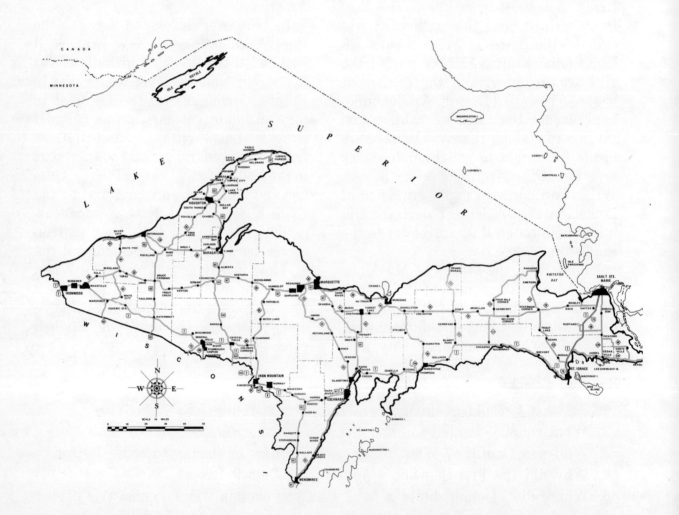

Michigan's Upper Peninsula. Larger cities are marked in black to show their approximate size. Maps are not the same scale.

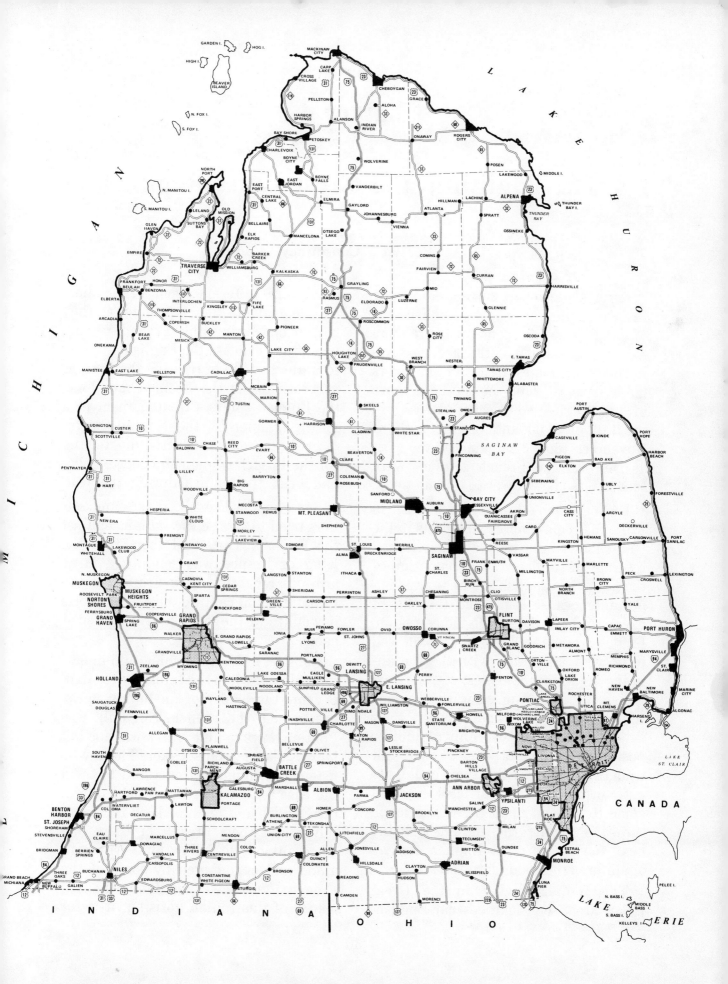

Michigan's Lower Peninsula.

Chapter 4

The English in the Great Lakes Region

Pontiac's Conspiracy

After the French surrendered New France to the English, the English sent Major Rogers with some of his rangers to take possession of the French forts in the Great Lakes area. Major Rogers made his way along the southern shore of Lake Erie and reached Detroit in the fall of 1760 and on the 29th of November took command of the post at Detroit. The French soldiers were sent as prisoners of war to Philadelphia.

During the following summer, in 1761, the remaining French posts in the Great Lakes area were also garrisoned by English soldiers. The occupation of the forts by English soldiers was important because it marked the end of French rule in the Great Lakes region. French traders were no longer allowed to go west and trade with the Indians in the area north and west of the Great Lakes. When spring came the Indians sought fur traders and brought their furs to the trading posts only to find the posts deserted and the French fur traders gone. Because they could not get powder and other articles they had come to depend upon there was much suffering among the Indians for the next few years until English traders again brought goods into the area.

The Indians, living in the Great Lakes area, soon learned that English-men were different from Frenchmen. No longer were they welcome, as they had been during the French period, when they came to the English outposts to trade. Instead of treating the Indians as brothers, as the French had done, the English soldiers treated them in a hostile manner for they feared the Indians because of their friendly feeling for the French traders and settlers who had been their allies during the war.

Some of the French traders and settlers tried to arouse the Indians against the English. They told them that the King of France was sending a large army to recapture New France. If the Indians would capture the English forts it would aid the French army when it came.

Pontiac, an Ottawa chief, and one of the ablest leaders the Indians ever had, became the leader of an Indian uprising to help the French. Not only was Pontiac a brave and crafty warrior but he was also a good speaker. Those who listened to him, as he pictured to them the ease with which they could defeat the English and take the land for themselves and their French brothers, became anxious to follow him. Although aided and encouraged by some of the French, Pontiac was, no doubt, the real leader of this Indian uprising. It is for

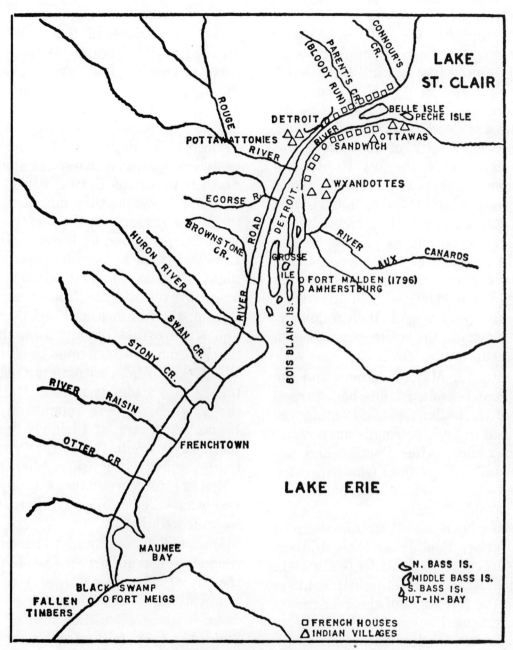

The Detroit River Area (1760-1815)

this reason that it is known to us as Pontiac's Conspiracy.

On April 27, 1763, a large band of Indians met at the Ecorse River, not far from Detroit. Indians were there from many of the leading tribes of the region. Pontiac made a long and forceful speech. In his talk he told his Indian brothers of the wrongs that they were suffering because of the English and pleaded with them to take up the hatchet and attack the English and thus aid the French army that was soon to come. So forceful was Pontiac's talk that many Indians were ready to join him and do as he wished. It was planned that the Indians would attack all of the posts at about the same time. In this way Pontiac hoped to keep the English soldiers from giving aid to each other.

At a certain time the Indians, living in the region near each of the forts, were to capture the fort and kill the English soldiers.

The first fort in Michigan to be attacked was Detroit. On May 7th, 1763, Pontiac with sixty of his chiefs was permitted to enter the fort. Hidden under their blankets the Indians carried guns from which the long barrels had been cut off. It was Pontiac's plan to make a speech and at its end he was to hold up a belt of wampum as a sign for the Indians with him to attack the garrison. The chiefs with Pontiac were to kill the soldiers while their followers, hidden outside the walls, were to rush in and capture the fort.

Luckily for Major Gladwin and the English at Detroit, friends had warned them of the Indians' plans. Pontiac was surprised to find the Englishmen ready for an attack. After Pontiac had finished talking, Major Gladwin then opened their blankets and pointed to their sawed-off guns.

Having been unable to take the post by surprise, Pontiac and his Indians then turned to siege and open attack. Fortunately for the English soldiers within the fort some of the French settlers remained loyal to them. From these French settlers the English soldiers and people in the stockade were able to get food all during the summer of 1763.

Late in June, Captain Dalyell reached Detroit with much needed supplies and men. Not being an experienced Indian fighter, or knowing the real strength of the Indians under Pontiac, Captain Dalyell planned to attack the Indian camp at night and thus break the Indians' power.

At two o'clock in the morning of July 31, 1763, Captain Dalyell led a force of two hundred fifty English soldiers out of the gate of the little fort. Following what was then a road, and has since become East Jefferson Avenue in Detroit, the English soldiers marched eastward for about two miles along the north bank of the Detroit River. Little did they know, as they marched along in the darkness, that their every move was being watched by Indian eyes that followed them in the blackness of the night. Just as the first soldiers were passing over a little bridge across a stream, then known as Parent's Creek and since called Bloody Run, the Indians began an attack upon the English. What was to be a surprise attack now turned into a bloody retreat. Gallantly the English soldiers fought off their Indian attackers and slowly worked their way back to the fort. During the battle seventy English soldiers were killed and forty wounded. Captain Dalyell was killed while trying to aid a wounded soldier.

Ensign Schlosser and fourteen men were stationed at Fort St. Joseph, where the city of Niles now stands. A band of Potawatomi, pretending friendship, came to the fort on the 25th of May. Suddenly they fell upon the soldiers and killed all of them except Ensign Schlosser and three others. These four men were later taken to Detroit where they were exchanged for Indian captives.

At the time of the Indian attack on the post of Michilimackinac the fort was located on the south side of the Straits of Mackinac at what is now Mackinaw City. The post was under the command of Major Etherington who had under him ninety-two soldiers. Four English fur traders were also living at the post. There were also a few French farmers living near the fort.

Although Major Etherington had been warned of the coming Indian attack upon the fort he disregarded the friendly warning. On the 2nd of June 1763, Indians who had been friendly to the English began gathering around the friendly, and as it was the king's birthday — a holiday — Major Etherington and his men left the fort unguarded and sat idly by, in the shade of the stockade, watching the game of lacrosse. When the game had gone on for some time, one of the Indians threw the ball high into the air and over the palisade. Into the fort rushed the Indians through the open gate. Indian women had placed

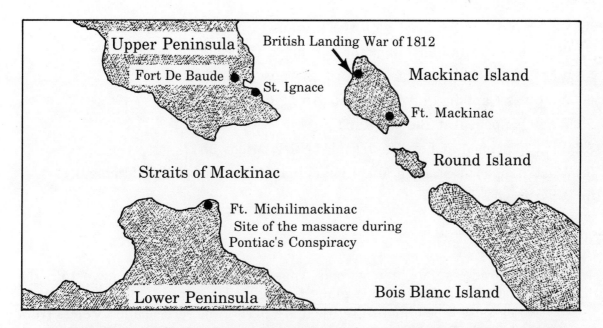

The name Michilimackinac applies to the whole Straits of Mackinac region. There are several major historic sites here. Father Marquette's mission and Fort de Buade were at St. Ignace in the late 1600s. The French built Fort Michilimackinac on the south side of the Straits about 1715. The British took over this fort in 1761; Indians captured it during Pontiac's Conspiracy in 1763. During the Revolutionary War, the British built a new, stronger fort on Mackinac Island. It was this fort, Fort Mackinac, the Americans took over in 1796. Though the British captured it in the War of 1812, it was returned to the U.S. at the war's end. Soldiers were stationed at Fort Mackinac until 1896. Both forts are now restored as part of state parks.

fort. They invited Major Etherington and the English soldiers to watch a game of lacrosse that was to be played between two Indian tribes. This was a favorite game of the Indians in which the players used a long-handled racket to catch, throw, or carry the ball into the opponent's goal.

Because the Indians seemed to be themselves nearby and handed the Indian warriors the guns and tomahawks they had carefully hidden under their blankets. Thus the Indians, having the fort within their power, fell upon the helpless English soldiers. All were killed except Major Etherington, three of the fur traders and twenty-three of the soldiers. These the Indians took prisoner and later released.

Most of the forts attacked by the Indians were taken by them. In spite of this success the plan of the Indians failed for they did not succeed in driving the English from the region. The following year, 1764, English armies came into the wilderness to punish the Indians and make peace with them. Before long the whole territory was again in the hands of the English.

Reading Checks

1. Why did the Indians dislike the English that came into their homeland?
2. How did the Frenchmen influence the thinking of the Indians in regard to the English?
3. Where did Pontiac meet with the Indians to plan his conspiracy?
4. What was the Indians' plan for capturing the English forts?
5. Who led the Indian attack against the post at Detroit?
6. Who was Captain Dalyell? What did he do?
7. What happened at Bloody Run?
8. What happened at Fort St. Joseph (Niles, Michigan)?
9. What happened at Fort Michilimackinac (Mackinaw City, Michigan)?
10. What is lacrosse?

Things to Do

1. A French trader's daughter, named Angeleque Cullerier, may have told the British about the Indian's plans to attack Detroit. If you can, listen to the cassette tape about this girl. It is a part of the series called **Voices from Michigan's Past.**
2. How did the Indians cut off the barrels of their guns? Did they have help to do this? Would this have tipped off the British?
3. Pontiac showed how powerful the Indians could be when they worked together. Discuss reasons why they didn't do this more often to get their way.

The Close of the English Period

England was in control of this area from 1760 to 1796. After Pontiac's uprising, few events of importance happened during the English period. Although the American Revolution took place during the years England held Michigan, this area was located too far from the scene of conflict to take an important part in the struggle. Some Indians did go east to fight with the English against the colonists.

During the war Detroit was the cen-

Michigan

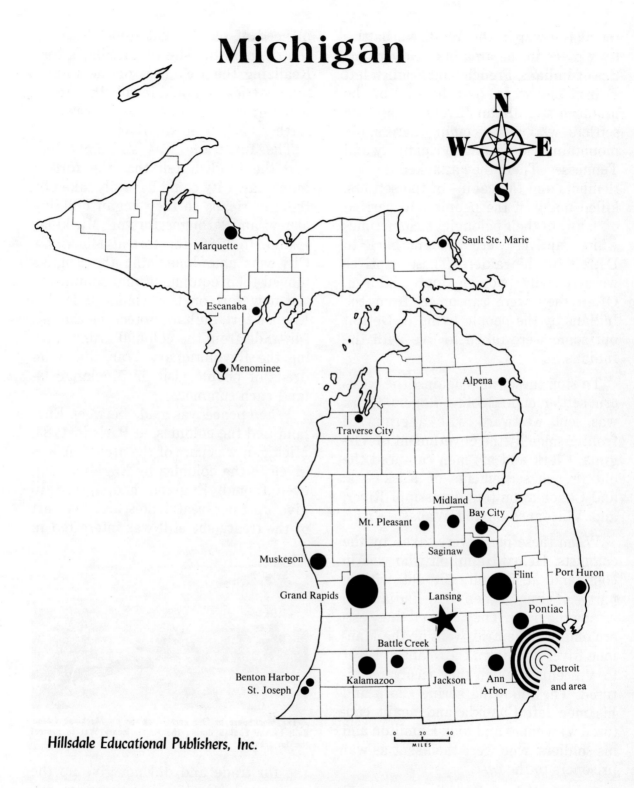

The main cities in Michigan today. The larger the dot the bigger the city. The capital is marked by a star.

Hillsdale Educational Publishers, Inc.

41

ter of the war in the West. No battles took place in the area but raiding parties of Indians, French, and English left Detroit and went south by way of the Maumee and Miami Rivers to raid the settlers who were coming across the mountains and settling in Kentucky and Tennessee. There they attacked the settlements and the cabins of the settlers, killed many of the people and carried off many of their belongings. Sometimes white captives were brought back to Detroit by the raiders. These captives were usually women and children. Often they were ransomed from the Indians by the people living in Detroit but some were taken to live with the Indians.

To stop these raids against the western settlements George Rogers Clark was sent westward with a group of frontiersmen by the government of Virginia. Clark and his men captured the old French settlements of Kaskaskia, and Cahokia, on the Mississippi River, and Vincennes on the Wabash River.

When these posts were taken by the colonists, Henry Hamilton who was in command at Detroit, set out with a party of Englishmen and Indians to retake the posts. They crossed the western end of Lake Erie, went up the Maumee River and down the Wabash River to Vincennes which they easily recaptured. The following spring Clark and his men left Cahokia and again captured Vincennes and took Hamilton and his soldiers, who were then sent as war prisoners to the east.

The English at Detroit were afraid that Clark and his men would come north and attack the fort. At that time it was a little wooden palisade, much

in need of repair, that stood down by the river on the site of Cadillac's fort. Realizing the weakness of the fort, if the Americans should invade the area, a new fort called Fort Lernoult, was built farther back from the river.

The fur trade was still important and the English felt that the fort at Mackinaw City could be easily taken by the Americans so they began building a new and stronger fort on Mackinac Island. In 1780, the fort at Mackinaw City was abandoned and the English moved their equipment and supplies to the new fort on the island. It is this English fort, built to protect the English fur trade from the colonial armies during the Revolutionary War, that hundreds of people visit on Mackinac Island each summer.

When peace was made between England and the colonies, at Paris in 1783, Michigan was part of the area that was given to the colonies by England. But, even though England had agreed to give up the Great Lakes area as part of the treaty she still was interested in

The blockhouse of Old Fort Mackinac on Mackinac Island. Built by the English during the Revolutionary War to protect the fur trade.

the fur trade and did not give up the posts until July 1796. At that time soldiers from the new United States came into the area to take over the posts from the English. As they came into the area they stopped at Monroe and there for the first time the United States flag was raised on what later became Michigan soil.

To Check Your Reading

1. What part did the people of Detroit play in the Revolutionary War?

2. Why did George Rogers Clark capture the posts on the Wabash and Mississippi Rivers?

3. Who was in command of the fort at Detroit when the war started? What happened to him?

4. Why did the English still hold the lake region until 1796?

5. Where was the first American flag raised in Michigan?

6. What two new forts were built at this time? Where were they located?

7. What route did Hamilton follow in going from Detroit to Vincennes?

Things to Do

1. Ask your librarian to help you find material about Simon Girty, Henry Hamilton, and the raids on the Kentucky and Tennessee settlers.

2. What does your United States history book tell you about George Rogers Clark and his men?

3. If your library has a history of Canada read what it says about the Revolutionary War.

4. Find out how a flintlock gun works. How has gunpowder developed over the years?

Map Work

1. Locate the old French settlements of Kaskaskia, Cahokia, and Vincennes.

2. Locate Detroit, Mackinaw City, Mackinac Island, and Niles where Fort St. Joseph was located.

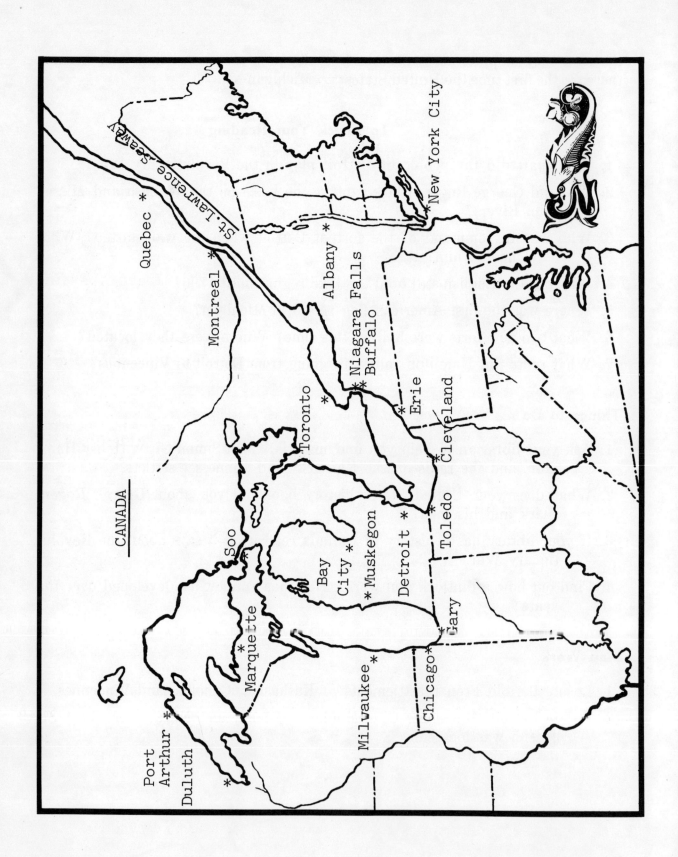

CANADA

St. Lawrence Seaway

Quebec *

Montreal *

Albany *

New York City *

Niagara Falls
Buffalo *

Toronto *

Erie *

Cleveland *

Soo *

Bay
City *

Muskegon *

Detroit *

Toledo *

Marquette *

Gary *

Milwaukee *

Chicago *

Port
Arthur *

Duluth *

Chapter 5

A Wilderness Area Becomes a State

The Ordinance of 1787

Although Michigan was included in the territory given to the United States at the close of the Revolutionary War, England still retained control of the area of the Great Lakes for some years after the war. However, the United States soon went ahead with plans for governing and developing the Northwest Territory. In 1787, the Continental Congress passed an ordinance, known as the Northwest Ordinance or the Ordinance of 1787, creating the Northwest Territory and providing a government for it. This new Northwest Territory included all the land north of the Ohio River and east of the Mississippi River, or what is today the states of Ohio, Indiana, Illinois, Michigan, Wisconsin, and a little of northeastern Minnesota. The ordinance passed to govern this territory was so well made that it has served as a model for the government of all later territories of the United States.

The Ordinance of 1787 made provision for territorial government to care for the settlers as they pushed west to occupy the area. It provided a governor for the area, a secretary, and three judges. Later when the area contained five thousand free male inhabitants they were to be able to elect their own General Assembly. This General Assembly, together with a Legislative Council of ten, chosen by Congress, was to pass laws, along with the governor, to govern the territory. What is more, the territory could elect a delegate to Congress who had the right to debate but not vote in that body.

In addition to the framework of government set up in the Ordinance of 1787 it also contained six important articles as follows:

Article one gave the settler the right to freedom of worship or religious sentiments as long as he conducted himself in a peaceful and orderly manner.

Article two contained a bill of rights, some of which were: That all settlers were entitled to a writ of habeas corpus, trial by jury, proportionate representation in the territorial legislature, the right to bail, no cruel punishments were to be inflicted, full compensation was to be given for property taken by the government, and the upholding of all private contracts.

Article three made the following statement regarding the importance of education: "Religion, morality, and knowledge being necessary to good government and the happiness of mankind, schools and the means of education shall forever be encouraged." Article three also stated that Indian lands and property were not to be taken from them without their consent.

Article four stated that the states formed from the territory were forever to remain a part of the United States and that all navigable waters leading to the Mississippi and St. Lawrence were to be common highways forever without tax or duty.

Article five states, "There shall be formed in the said territory, not less than three nor more than five states." The ordinance established in general terms what these five states were to be and further said that "whenever any of the said States shall have sixty thousand free inhabitants therein, such State shall be admitted—into the Congress of the United States on an equal footing with the original States. . . ."

Article six provided that "there shall be neither slavery nor involuntary servitude in the said territory, otherwise than in the punishment of crimes whereof the party shall have been duly convicted." This article thus excluded slavery from the Northwest Territory.

Can You Answer These?

1. What was the Ordinance of 1787? What body passed this ordinance?

2. What states have been cut from the Old Northwest Territory?

3. What system of government did it set up for the area?

4. What provisions did the articles contain?

5. What did it say about 1. freedom of worship, 2. civil rights, 3. education, 4. commerce on the St. Lawrence and Mississippi rivers, 5. the number of states to be made from the area, and 6. about slavery?

6. What is the difference between a territory and a state? Are there still parts of the United States that aren't states?

Map Work

1. On a map of the United States be able to point out the area included in the Northwest Territory.

2. Locate the five states that make up the old Northwest Territory; locate the Ohio, Mississippi, and St. Lawrence rivers. Put these on your outline map.

A New System of Land Survey

In order to give each of the new settlers who would come into the Northwest Territory a clear title to his land, the congress set up a new system of surveying land. All the land in the Northwest Territory was to be divided into Congressional, or geographical, townships; each one was to be six miles square. This would make a map of the area look somewhat like a large checkerboard.

In Michigan these squares, called

Congressional Townships, were to be measured east and west from a principal meridian that runs north and south through the state at 84 degrees, 22 minutes and 24 seconds west longitude. They were to be numbered north and south of a base line that now forms the Eight Mile Road, or the northern boundary of Wayne County, and is located at 42 degrees, 26 minutes, and 30 seconds north latitude. If you will look at a map of Michigan you will see that this line forms the northern boundary of the second row of counties.

Here is an example — see the next page also.

If a farmer settled on land in township W his title would be described as being in township 4 North, Range 6 West. No other township in the state can give this same location. Township

X would be described as township 3 South, Range 6 East; Y as township 1 South, Range 2 West; Z as township 3 North, Range 4 East.

To locate a township was well but a township six miles square in size contains thirty-six square miles. In each township there are 23,040 acres of land. Such farms were too large for the early Michigan farmer. With the tools he had, forty or eighty acres of land was large enough for a farm.

In order to locate these little pieces of land each township was again divided into thirty-six smaller parts like a smaller checkerboard.

Thus the entire state was divided into areas one mile square. Each of these squares was called a section. It takes thirty-six of these sections to make one township. All townships are numbered

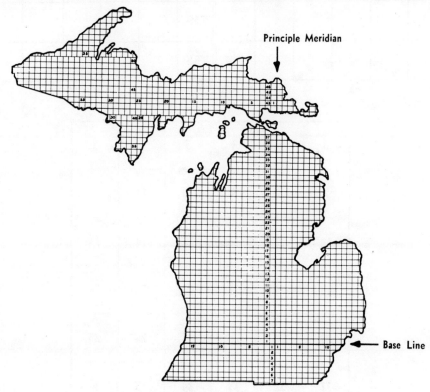

Map showing Congressional Townships

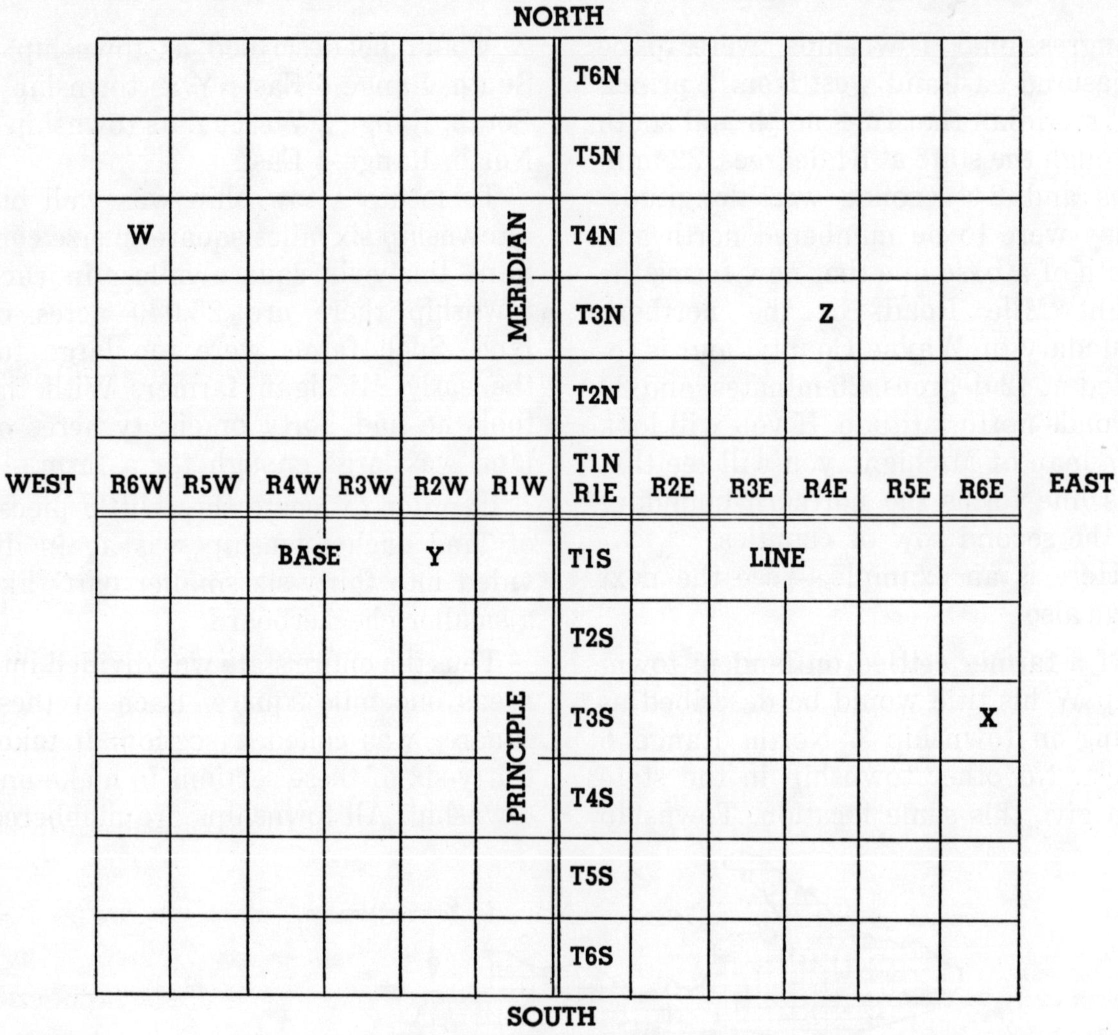

NORTH

	R6W	R5W	R4W	R3W	R2W	R1W	T·N / R·E	R2E	R3E	R4E	R5E	R6E	
							T6N						
							T5N						
	W						T4N						
							T3N			Z			
							T2N						
WEST	R6W	R5W	R4W	R3W	R2W	R1W	T1N / R1E	R2E	R3E	R4E	R5E	R6E	EAST
			BASE		Y		T1S		LINE				
							T2S						
							T3S					X	
							T4S						
							T5S						
							T6S						

PRINCIPLE MERIDIAN

SOUTH

6	5	4	3	2	1
7	8	9	10	11	12
18	17	16	15	14	13
19	20	21	22	23	24
30	29	28	27	26	25
31	32	33	34	35	36

48

like the one on p. 47. Each of these sections contains 640 acres of land and can be divided in the following manner to locate smaller pieces of land.

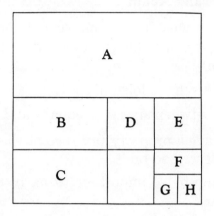

A is described as the north one half of section (1. 2. 10.) or any other section of a definite township and contains 320 acres.

B is described as the north one half of the southwest one fourth and has eighty acres.

C is described as the south one half of the southwest one fourth and has eighty acres.

D is described as the northwest one fourth of the southeast one fourth and has forty acres.

E is described as the northeast one fourth of the southeast one fourth and has forty acres.

F is described as the north one half of the southeast one fourth of the southeast one fourth and has twenty acres.

G is described as the southwest one fourth of the southeast one fourth of the southeast one fourth and has ten acres.

H is described as the southeast one fourth of the southeast one fourth of the southeast one fourth and has ten acres.

How Well Did You Read?

1. What body set up a new system of land survey for the Northwest Territory?
2. How many miles square are congressional townships?
3. Congressional townships are measured north and south of what line? Where is this line located?
4. Congressional townships are measured east and west of what line?
5. How many acres are there in a congressional township?
6. How many sections are there in a township?
7. How many acres are there in a section of land?

8. How many acres are there in one-half section? in a quarter section?

Things to Do, Find, and Talk About

1. In what congressional township is your school located? Can you find this township on a map? Count off the townships from the base line and the principal meridian.

2. In what section is your school located?

3. What is the difference between six miles square and six square miles?

4. Perhaps your parents have a property tax receipt they can show you. See how their property is described on it.

5. Why would land location be so important to early pioneers? What problems did maps have then?

Map Work

1. You may have asked yourself what use is the township location system. It can be used to exactly locate land for many purposes. The book, **Minerology of Michigan,** by E. W. Heinrich, tells where many minerals have been found. It gives the location of a former gold mine as NE¼ SEC. 35T48N, R28W. Locate this on a map. The directions show a ½ mile square in which the mine is located.

Michigan Becomes a Territory

In 1800 the Northwest Territory was divided into two territories. The Lower Peninsula of Michigan was divided into two parts by a line running north and south near the center of the state. While the eastern part of the Lower Peninsula remained with Ohio as part of the old Northwest Territory, the western half of the Lower Peninsula and nearly all of the Upper Peninsula became part of a new territory called Indiana Territory.

In 1803, when Ohio became a separate state, all of Michigan became part of the Indiana Territory. This plan was not pleasing to the people living in Michigan so a new and separate territory of Michigan was soon made.

On January 11, 1805, Congress passed an act which made Michigan a separate territory known as Michigan Territory. This territory was made up of what is now the Lower Peninsula, and a little of the eastern part of the Upper Peninsula. General Hull, an old Revolutionary War soldier, was made governor of the new territory. In July 1805, General Hull arrived at Detroit to begin his duties as governor of Michigan Territory. When General Hull arrived he was shocked. He found that Detroit had been destroyed by a fire, and that the people were then living in little camps in the open fields.

On the morning of June 11, 1805, a baker named John Harvey needed to get some flour from the little mill, on May's Creek, which used to stand near where the Amtrack station now stands in Detroit. He hitched his pony to his small two wheeled cart but before climbing upon the seat he stopped to knock the ashes from his pipe because the wind was blowing the ashes in his face. As the lighted tobacco fell from his pipe it was caught by the strong wind and blown through the open doorway into the barn. There it scattered and quickly caught some hay on fire.

The flames, fanned by a strong wind, quickly spread from building to building. As all of the buildings were made of wood, the whole town was soon in flames. When night came all that was left were a few smoking ruins. The people who lived in Detroit were homeless. Many found shelter and food with friends that lived along both sides of the river.

Father Gabriel Richard, then pastor of Ste. Anne's Church, saw the need of the people. Under his leadership men were sent up and down the river in canoes to call on the farmers and bring food and help to the homeless people.

Plans for a new city were soon made. They were drawn much like those of the new capital city of Washington, D.C., which was then being built. The streets were to be much wider than they had been before. Some of the main streets were to spread out like the spokes in a wheel. Although this plan was not exactly carried out, some of it was. Several of Detroit's downtown streets go back to this plan that was made after the fire in 1805.

To Check Your Reading

1. Michigan became a territory in what year?

2. Who became governor of the new Michigan territory?

3. What happened at Detroit on June 11, 1805?

4. Who was Father Gabriel Richard?

5. The plans for the new city of Detroit were to be similar to those of what other city?

6. How large was the new Michigan Territory? See the **Atlas of Michigan,** p. 114-6 to learn how the boundaries of the territory changed and developed.

The War of 1812

When General Hull came to Michigan Territory, there were less than four thousand people living here. The entire area was still a forest land. The only areas that could be called settled were Detroit, Frenchtown (Monroe), and Niles. A few people were living in the Straits of Mackinac area at St. Ignace, at Mackinaw City, and on Mackinac Island. Detroit was still a small place with only about seventeen hundred people.

Although settlers were coming into southern Ohio, Indiana, and Illinois, only a few came to Michigan. None of the land had been surveyed or put up

51

for sale. The Erie Canal had not yet been built and it was still difficult to get to Michigan or to send farm produce back to the markets in the East.

Because of the fear of war with England, General Hull was given, in the spring of 1812, a military force to protect the frontier from attack by the Canadians and Indians. Leaving Dayton, Ohio, General Hull and his soldiers marched north through the forests of Ohio toward Detroit. The progress of the soldiers was very slow because they had to clear much of the road through the forest as they came northward. A large swamp area around present day Toledo, known as the Black Swamp, was very difficult to cross. When General Hull and his soldiers reached Detroit, war between England and the United States had already started.

Below Detroit, on the Canadian side of the river, the English had built a small fort named Fort Malden. It was located at what is now Amherstburg, Ontario. From Fort Malden English troops could be sent across the Detroit River to block the only road between Detroit and the Ohio settlements.

General Hull received orders to cross the Detroit River and capture Fort Malden. This would then give the Americans control of much of Upper Canada. Instead of advancing at once upon the Canadian fort, Hull did not set out until the 12th of July. Even then he did not hurry. A sudden attack might have helped the Americans to have taken the fort. At that time Fort Malden was garrisoned by only a few English soldiers. Almost a month passed, yet General Hull waited. During this time the English were busy preparing for an attack upon the

fort at Detroit. Soldiers, under the command of General Brock, arrived from the East to strengthen the English soldiers already at Fort Malden. On August the 9th General Hull gave up his plans to capture Fort Malden and occupy Canada. Recrossing the Detroit River he and his men again entered the fort at Detroit.

General Brock, the day following his arrival at Fort Malden, set out to capture the American post at Detroit. Under the command of Brock were about thirteen hundred men while the American army under Hull numbered less than a thousand. The English took Detroit with not a shot being fired by the American forces. Colonel Proctor was placed in command of the area.

On July 16, 1812, British soldiers arrived at Mackinac Island and climbed a hill high above the fort. They hauled a cannon up with them. The Americans in the fort were outnumbered and surprised. They realized that the British could shell the fort at their leisure and there was little they could do to stop them. Surrender seemed the only way out.

The Americans, however, were not to give up the struggle in the Lake Region. General Harrison began the building of an army to drive out the English. While still encamped at Sandusky, Ohio, General Harrison sent out a small party of men, under General Winchester, to act as an advance guard. On the cold winter night of January 22, 1813, Winchester and his men were camped at Frenchtown (Monroe) on the River Raisin. Here they were attacked by English soldiers and Indians from Fort Malden.

The Americans had been very careless about placing guards about their camp and had not listened to the warnings of the white settlers or friendly Indians. Part of the American forces were soon killed and the rest were forced to surrender. The wounded men were left behind at Frenchtown while the prisoners, that were able to walk, were marched over the ice of the Detroit River to Fort Malden.

During the night of the 23rd of January, 1813, the Indians became drunk and many of them returned to Frenchtown. The old fur storage houses where the wounded Americans had been placed were set on fire. If a soldier was successful in reaching the door, in an attempt to escape from the flames, he was dragged out and cruelly murdered. Because of this cruelty of the Indians, the Americans increased their efforts to retake the Lake Region and punish the Indians. The battle cry "Remember the Raisin" became the slogan of the American armies sent into the Lake Region.

Because of the lack of good roads it was necessary for the Americans to gain control of the lakes before they could again control Michigan. On the south shore of Lake Erie, at what is now Erie, Pennsylvania, a few boats were built by the Americans. This little fleet was placed under the command of Commodore Perry. When the American ships appeared on Lake Erie the English naval commander, Captain Barclay, gathered his ships at Fort Malden where they could have the protection of the guns of the fort. Perry's force was not strong enough to face the guns of both the English ships and the fort, so he waited at Put-in-Bay in the Bass Islands until the English ships should appear on the lake to drive the Americans from it.

Perry did not have long to wait because the English, in order to hold the Lake Region, must control Lake Erie so that supplies for the soldiers, prisoners, and Indians could be brought to Fort Malden from the East. On the morning of September 13, 1813, Captain Barclay with six ships and about five hundred men, set sail for Put-in-Bay to drive the American ships from the lake.

At nine o'clock the American lookout at Put-in-Bay saw the sails of the English ships coming across the water. Perry got his ships ready for action and set out to meet the English ships. As there was little wind on that day, the two squadrons came toward each other very slowly. About noon, the ships of the English and Americans were close enough together so that their guns could be used. For three hours the battle went on. The Americans finally defeated the English.

Colonel Proctor, now cut off from his base of supplies in the East, abandoned Fort Malden and Detroit, much to the anger of the Indians under Tecumseh, and began a retreat across Canada to the East.

At Moravian Town, in Canada, not far from Chatham, Ontario, Proctor's fleeing army was overtaken by the Americans under Harrison. A battle, known as the Battle of the Thames, followed in which the English army was defeated, and the able Indian leader Tecumseh was killed.

On the 29th of September the Americans re-entered the fort at Detroit. On the 9th of the following month, Lewis Cass was appointed governor of the territory. In 1814 an unsuccessful attempt was made to recapture Fort Michilimackinac, from the English, but it was not until after the War of 1812 was over that the Americans again took possession of that post.

How Well Did You Read?

1. What was Michigan like in 1812?

2. Where was Fort Malden located? Can you find Amherstburg, Ontario, on a map of Ontario, Canada?

3. Who was General Brock?

4. What happened at Fort Mackinac, on Mackinac Island?

5. What happened at Frenchtown (Monroe)? What battle cry was used after this?

6. Who was Commodore Perry and what did he do?

7. Who became the new governor of Michigan Territory?

8. Who was Tecumseh? (See **Tecumseh's Last Stand** by John Sugden. 1986)

Things to Do and Talk About

1. Does your library have any material on Perry and his victory on Lake Erie? (See **American History Illustrated** — July, 1967.)

2. What material can you find about Tecumseh?

3. Find out more about Hull's surrender of Detroit. Did he have any good reasons?

4. If you live near the Straits of Mackinac, visit the Fort on Mackinac Island.

5. How is Thames correctly pronounced? Where is the other Thames River?

Map Work

1. On a wall map in your room be able to locate the River Raisin, Maumee Bay, Fort Malden, Put-in-Bay, Thames River, Erie (Pennsylvania), Mackinac Island, Bass Islands, Frenchtown (Monroe), and the place where the Battle of the Thames was fought.

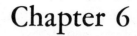
A canal boat

Chapter 6

The Settlement of Southern Michigan

The Erie Canal Made a Waterway to the Great Lakes

In 1817, the state of New York began the building of a canal to run east and west across the state from Albany, on the Hudson River, to Buffalo, on Lake Erie. This new canal was named the Erie Canal. It was 363 miles long and was completed in 1825. The canal was forty feet wide at the top, twenty-eight feet wide at the bottom and had a minimum depth of four feet.

Before 1825, there had been no easy way to bring goods into the Great Lakes area or to take goods to the eastern cities. Now a water route by means of the canal and the Great Lakes led all the way from New York City, on the Hudson River, to far off Chicago, at the southern end of Lake Michigan.

Soon canal boats, drawn by horses, or mules, were carrying people and freight of all kinds between Albany and Buffalo. Some of the canal boats carried freight while others, called packet boats, carried only passengers. Now that a good means of transportation had developed hundreds of people left the state of New York and the poorer lands of New England and came west, by means of the canal, to start new farms on the better lands in the West. Many of them were Quakers. A few of the early settlers in Washtenaw County were free Blacks who came from the East to start farms along with the others.

Route of Erie Canal

Settlers coming to Michigan could cross New York State from Albany to Buffalo on the Erie Canal. From there they could come across Canada to Windsor, Ontario, come across northern Ohio, south of Lake Erie, or take one of the sailboats or new passenger steamers, at Buffalo and cross Lake Erie to Monroe or Detroit.

Some of the early settlers in southwestern Michigan came north from Ohio and Indiana. But most of the settlers in southern Michigan came across New York State along the Genesee Road or on the Erie Canal.

The Erie Canal not only made it easier for settlers to reach Michigan but also provided an easy way for settlers to send their goods; such as, wheat, corn, smoked hams, and poultry to market, allowing them to make more money farming. Because of the traffic on the canal the city of New York grew rapidly in size.

Can You Answer These?

1. Across what state did the Erie Canal run?

2. What two cities, in New York state, did the canal connect?

3. What were packet boats?

4. How did the Erie Canal affect the settlement of the Great Lakes area?

Things to Do and Talk About

1. Can you find out more about the Erie Canal in the books in your library? Tell the class about what you have read. (See **Am. History Illust.** August 1972.)

2. Read **Vanishing Landscape** by Eric Sloan, especially p. 49.

3. Can you find any pictures of the Erie Canal, canal boats, or canal locks in your history books or in the books in the library?

4. Why could canal boats carry freight cheaper than horse drawn wagons?

5. What can you find out about the Conestoga wagon as a freight carrier?

6. Use the Michigan Atlas to compare the number of new settlers coming from other states versus those from overseas.

Map Work

1. Be able to trace the route of the Erie Canal on a large map in your classroom.

How the Early Settlers Lived

At the time Michigan was first being settled most of the people in the United States were farmers so most of the people who came here to live came to start new farms. However, there were some crafts people who also came to Michigan and settled in the little villages that were developing in the southern part of the state. There were carpenters, blacksmiths, harness makers, wheelwrights, coopers, cobblers, gunsmiths, and shipwrights.

Many of the settlers walked all the way from their homes in the East to Michigan. Most of them, however, used a wagon to carry a few household items and the few tools they possessed; such as, pots and kettles, a grinding stone, a loom, an axe, an adze, and an auger. If they came across Lake Erie the wagons were driven onto one of the boats. Then the wheels of the wagons were taken from the wagon axles and securely fastened to the side of the boat so that they would not roll around if the boat pitched during a storm. Often the settlers lived in their wagons as they came across Lake Erie. When they arrived at Detroit, or Monroe, the wheels were put back onto the wagons. When the wagons had been taken off the boat, the horses or oxen, were then hitched to them. With their things piled inside the wagon and perhaps a cow or two tied on behind, and a lean dog running under the wagon, the settlers passed through the streets of Detroit, or Monroe, and on out into the state on one of the new roads that were then being cut through the forest.

The Chicago Road led west across the state through the southernmost row of counties. The Territorial Road ran west through the second row of counties. The Grand River Road ran northwest to the Grand River at what is now Lansing. Another road, now called Woodward Avenue in Detroit, ran north toward Saginaw. The Fort Gratiot Road ran to Fort Gratiot, now Port Huron. It was over these roads that the early settlers pushed out into Michigan's forest lands.

The roads were rough and often muddy from Detroit. Sometimes a loaded wagon would get stuck in the mud. Usually there were other settlers coming along the road and they helped each other along the way. At night the settlers camped beside the road or stayed at one of the few inns that were being built to care for travelers. At last, after many days of traveling, the settlers reached the place where they were going to build their homes and clear the land that was to become their farm.

The first task of a settler was the building of a log cabin that the family would call their home. Trees, about a foot in diameter, were cut and made ready to be used in building the cabin. When the logs were ready, neighbors came to help the new settler build his little one room log cabin. These house raisings were called bees. These bees were one of the social occasions of that time. It was not uncommon for a man to walk twenty miles to help his new neighbor build his home. All that was asked of the new settler for this kindness was that he help others who would come later and settle in the area.

These little log cabins were built of round logs and usually were no larger than one small room. Glass was too expensive for most of the early settlers and so their cabins had no windows. The only light to enter would be let in by the open door. For shingles the settlers used bark but this was soon replaced by homemade shingles called shakes. These shakes kept the water out of the cabins, but the holes between them easily let out the warm air. In the winter, during a storm, fine snow would often be blown into the room.

Every cabin had a fireplace made of sticks and clay. First two forms for the fireplace and chimney were made of small sticks. One was placed inside the other. As the forms went upward the settler packed clay in between them. Then it was allowed to dry. When it was finished and a fire was started in the fireplace the heat baked the clay into a hard tile. The sticks on the inside of the fireplace and chimney caught on fire and burned away but those on the outside helped to keep the baked clay in place. If the chimney cracked it was repaired with more clay. These early fireplaces provided little heat and settlers had to dress in warm clothing to keep warm and well during the wintertime. All the cooking was done over the little fire in the fireplace. At night the reddish glow from the fire, with perhaps a candle or two, was all the light the settlers had.

In these one room log cabins the entire family lived. Here the meals were cooked and eaten. Here neighbors and new settlers were entertained. In it the family found shelter during the night, from rain, snow, and the cold of winter. This one room, often very small, served all the purposes of our larger houses of today. Later these early log cabins were replaced by ones made from logs that were hewn by hand so that they were square. These houses, made of square timbers, were known as block houses. As the years passed and the farmers prospered, farm homes were made of lumber sawed in the many sawmills that were built in Michigan, or brick that was made in a local brickyard.

Clearing the land, so that crops could be planted was a difficult task, for the early settlers had few tools. In order that food for the family could be raised the first year the settlers often girdled the trees in Indian fashion to kill them. This they did by cutting a band in the bark all the way around the tree near the bottom. This kept the sap from going up the tree and the leaves soon died and fell to the ground. This let the sunlight in among the trees. Among the dead trees the early settlers planted their first crop. Usually it was corn but

sometimes wheat was also planted.

Each year the settlers would try to clear a little more land. Soon open fields, fenced with a split rail fence, were appearing near the cabins in what for ages had been only a vast forest land. The trees were cut down. Then the tree tops were cut up and piled on top of several tree trunks that had been dragged together. Then the whole was left to dry. In the fall the pile was set on fire. The settlers also used fire to get the stumps out of the ground. Thus, much of Michigan's valuable hardwood, in the southern part of the state, was burned.

When the land was ready for planting, the settlers prepared it for the seed by spading it by hand, or by plowing it with a crude wooden plow drawn by a team of oxen, or horses, if they were fortunate enough to own them. All the work of caring for the growing crops, as well as their harvesting, was done by the hard working settlers with crude homemade tools. Grain was cut with a sickle, or scythe. Then it was raked with a wooden rake and bound by hand into sheaves. These were placed in little piles called shocks and the grain was then left to dry, or cure, in the field. Then it was threshed by hand by the settlers using a flail. After it was winnowed the grain was ground either at home or at a local grist mill to which the farmer took his grain.

The duties of the early frontier women were many and hard. Not only must they care for their cabins and cook the meals but they must also do the washing, make soap and candles, mend the clothing, knit stockings, weave cloth, and make clothing. Often the frontier women toiled long into the night, by the flickering light of the fireplace, in order that the family could be fed and kept warm and happy.

Boys and girls of that day had little if any schooling. Sometimes they learned how to read and write, but that is all, for as soon as they were old enough to work they were given tasks to do.

Sickness or misfortune came to the settlers and their families many times. Often the little cabins were far from each other. Doctors were few and poorly educated. So the settlers learned to rely upon their own medical remedies. To provide medicine herbs were gathered in the summer and fall. These the settlers dried.

Around the little cabins lurked dangers against which the settlers must ever be on guard. Bears and wolves often attacked the animals of the settlers. Hawks carried off the settlers' poultry.

Although the life of the frontier settlers was a hard and dangerous one it was not without its amusements. Church going, weddings, house raisings, house warmings and husking bees were eagerly attended by everyone. Sometimes when there was less work to do the settlers visited each other just as we do today.

To Check Your Reading

1. By what routes did settlers come to Michigan?

2. What main roads led out from Detroit into the state?

3. Many of the early settlers in the southern part of the state came from what states or what part of the country?

4. What were the roads like at this time? Where did the settlers stay at night?

5. What were the early log cabins like?

6. How was the land cleared and prepared for crops?

7. Why did the settlers have to wear warm clothing indoors during the winter?

8. What were some of the tasks that the women had to do?

9. What amusements did the early settlers have? What was a bee?

Things to Do and Talk About

1. What materials can you find in your library that tell you more about early pioneer life in Michigan? The **Foxfire** books by Eliot Wigginton have a lot of information about pioneer life.

2. Would you like to have been an early settler in Michigan? Give your reasons why or why not. What advantages do we have today?

3. If there is a museum near your home that has pioneer tools or utensils on display go and visit it. Look at Eric Sloane's book, **Reverence of Wood.** It may give you some ideas for models of old tools you could build.

4. If you have any pioneer articles at home bring them to school and tell the class how they were used.

Early Statehood

By 1835 the people of Michigan Territory thought that there were enough people living here to entitle it to be made a state and admitted to the Union. A convention was held, and a regular constitution for the new state was made. After choosing Stevens T. Mason as the first governor, Michigan asked Congress to admit it to the union. The request of Michigan for statehood caused a dispute to arise between Michigan and Ohio over the boundary between the two states.

The current Capitol in Lansing was built in the 1870s. This drawing was made when the cornerstone was laid in 1873.

In 1803, Ohio had been admitted to the Union as a state. At that time the northern boundary of Ohio had not been definitely settled. In 1805, when Michigan Territory was organized, a line running due east from the most southern point of Lake Michigan was made the southern boundary of the new territory. According to this line, the City of Toledo and a large strip of northern Ohio were included in Michigan Territory. In 1835, Governor Lucas, of Ohio, took steps to organize this land as part of the State of Ohio. This action was promptly opposed by Governor Mason, of the Michigan Territory. The Michigan militia was sent to Toledo to prevent the Ohio governor from proceeding with his plans. Shots were exchanged between the two parties but no one was injured.

This dispute between Michigan and Ohio is known as the Toledo War.

So in 1835, when Michigan asked to become a state, Ohio opposed her request in Congress, claiming that it would not be wise to allow Michigan to come in until the northern boundary of Ohio had been settled. The dispute lasted for two years.

Congress settled the matter by giving the disputed territory, including Toledo, to the State of Ohio. Soon after this, on January 26, 1837, Michigan was admitted to the Union as a state.

To repay Michigan for the strip of land across the southern part of the Lower Peninsula, Congress gave Michigan the Upper Peninsula west of St. Ignace. At first, the people of the territory thought that they had received by far the poorer end of the bargain. But, when copper and iron ore were discovered in the Upper Peninsula many people changed their minds.

(For more information about the "Toledo War" read *The Rise and Fall of Toledo, Michigan,* by Mary Karl George.)

To Check Your Reading

1. Who was chosen to be the first governor of Michigan?

2. What was the Toledo War? What was it about?

3. Which state got the disputed territory?

4. When was Michigan admitted to the Union as a state?

5. How did Michigan get the area now known as the Upper Peninsula?

6. What did people think about getting the Upper Peninsula in exchange for the Toledo strip? Why did they later change their opinion regarding the value of the Upper Peninsula? Some people in the U.P. want to form their own state. Do you feel this would be a good idea?

(See *Superior — A State For The North Country* by Carter. — 1980)

The community works together to help build a barn for a friend. (Clark Historical Library, Central Michigan University)

Chapter 7

Slavery and the Underground Railroad

Slavery in the Old Northwest Territory

During the French and English occupation of Michigan some slaves were held in the area. The Ordinance of 1787, that you have read about, stated that there was to be no slavery in the Northwest Territory although it did provide for the return of runaway slaves to their masters if they were found in the area. But the ordinance did not apply in the area until 1796 when the area was transferred to the United States by Jay's treaty. Although the Ordinance of 1787 forbade slavery in the Northwest Territory, Jay's treaty upheld the property rights of the English and French people then living in the area. This meant that if they owned slaves at that time they were permitted to keep them. In 1792, the Canadian government had abolished slavery in Canada but this act seems to have been disregarded on the Michigan frontier.

By 1787, many slaves were already escaping from the South and fleeing to freedom in the North where they were aided by people who opposed slavery, especially the Quakers who felt that there was a higher law than those on the statute books of the nation.

Both the United States constitution and the Ordinance of 1787 provided for the return of runaway slaves to their masters. To stop people from aiding runaway slaves congress passed in 1793, the first Fugitive Slave Law. The law permitted a slave owner, or his agent, to seize the fugitive and return him, or her, to the rightful owner. It also provided a $500.00 fine and a prison term for anyone who hindered the arrest, harbored, or rescued an escaping slave.

In 1793, the same year that the Fugitive Slave Law was passed, Eli Whitney invented the cotton gin. Up to this time cotton had not been a major crop in the South but now that the seeds could be easily removed from the fiber it soon became one of the major cash crops grown in the South. This new crop required many field hands and the demand for more and more slaves grew as the volume of the crop increased.

The Beginning of the Antislavery Movement in Michigan

About the time Michigan became a state many people in the North, and some in the South, began to regard slavery as an evil institution that not only degraded blacks but white people as well.

From 1619 to 1808 blacks were brought from Africa to the southern

62

part of the United States and there sold as slaves to do the field work on the plantations in the South where rice, indigo, tobacco and cotton were grown. There were also a few blacks who were slaves in the North but slavery did not fit into the economy of the small self-sufficient farms, the newly developing industries, and the growing overseas shipping of the North. The few slaves found in the North were usually employed as domestic servants who served wealthy families.

Escaped slaves began coming to Michigan soon after the War of 1812. As the slaves continued to escape and tell of the harsh slavery conditions in the South an anti-slavery feeling slowly grew in the North. Although Michigan was to become a leader in the anti-slavery movement the status of blacks in Michigan was a problem to the early settlers. In 1827, the Territorial Legislature passed an act regarding blacks living in the territory. According to this act blacks were not residents or persons with civil rights. They were to possess a legal document stating that he, or she, was a free black. They were also to register with the county clerk and post a $500.00 bond for good behavior. Most of the early black settlers were descendants of blacks who had gained their freedom by fighting in the colonial army during the Revolutionary War or had been able to purchase their freedom from their masters. Few people of that day, even the white settlers, had $500.00 and legal certificates were easily lost or destroyed. The census of 1830 lists 22 male blacks and 16 female blacks as slaves and 139 free black males and 102 free female blacks then living in Michigan.

An important leader in the early anti-slavery movement in Michigan was a young woman named Elizabeth Margaret Chandler, who came to Lenawee County along with many Quaker settlers. A group of Quakers, in October 1832, under the leadership of Miss Chandler, organized the first anti-slavery society in Michigan Territory in a Quaker meeting house at Adrian in the Raisin River valley.

By 1833, when there took place in Detroit what was called "the Negro Riot," there were already several people who had strong feelings against slavery. An escaped slave, named Blackburn, and his wife, were arrested and were to be returned to their owner in the South. Mrs. Blackburn escaped from the jail. When the sheriff and his guard tried to take Mr. Blackburn to a steamboat on the river they were attacked by both blacks and whites. Mr. Blackburn was rescued and then taken with his wife across the Detroit River to freedom in Canada.

In 1834, Erotius Parmalee Hastings organized the first anti-slavery society group in Detroit. Another important leader in the anti-slavery movement was Laura Haviland whose statue now stands in front of the city hall at Adrian, Michigan. In 1839, she and her brother opened a co-educational school that was open to whites, Indians, and blacks. This was a very progressive movement for that time.

In 1836, a group of people met in the Presbyterian church in Ann Arbor and started the Michigan Anti-Slavery Society. The following year when Michigan became a state, in 1837, there were several free blacks and escaped slaves already living in the area. Some free blacks, as has already been told, came with the first white settlers. Blacks were living in Lenawee, Washtenaw, Cass, and Wayne counties. But they like the Indians were not given the right to vote under the new state constitution. The census of 1840 lists 753 blacks then living in Michigan.

The Underground Railroad

As the years passed, many Quakers and others who were against slavery gradually organized a way to aid slaves who were trying to escape from their masters and reach free territory. This group of people, together with their activities, began to be known as the Underground Railway (because it was secret) although it was not underground or a railway. It operated for about twenty or thirty years just before the Civil War.

The area south of the Ohio River was slave territory and escaping slaves had first to cross the river to get into free territory. Some southern whites, especially Quakers, often aided slaves to escape from their masters, cross the river, and find refuge with one of the members of the Underground Railroad who lived north of the river. Members of the Underground Railroad lived in the South, Pennsylvania, Ohio, Indiana, Illinois, southern Michigan and New York State.

Places where the escaping slaves were hidden were known as stations and the people who hid them were called agents. Once an escaping slave reached a station he, or she, was fed and given clothing if needed. Usually escaping slaves arrived at an agent's house in the middle of the night. But whatever the time, they were fed and cared for by the agent from his own personal supplies. To do this was against the Fugitive Slave Act of 1793 but members of the Underground Railroad felt it to be their moral duty to help slaves escape to freedom. Some agents were caught and lost their homes and farms as a result of their Underground Railroad activities.

When an escaping slave reached an agent's home he was hidden in a barn, attic, haystack, cellar, corn crib, wood lot, or any place where he could not be found by southerners looking for the runaway. They were usually passed along to the next station during the night. People who took the escapees to the next station were known as conductors. Usually the next station was not more than fifteen miles away so that the distance could be covered both ways in a single night. Sometimes the escaping slaves followed the conductor as he walked along back farm fences away from the dogs around farm houses, through woods or swamps, or corn fields. Often the path led up a stream, or along the shore of a lake, so bloodhounds could not follow. At other times, especially in the daytime, they were hidden in wagons under hay or straw, or under bags filled with straw to make them look as if they were filled with grain.

As the Underground Railway developed, several routes became main lines. Sometimes two alternate routes were used in order to make it more difficult for escaping slaves to be followed by slave catchers. One of the main routes from Kentucky, through Ohio, became known as the "Quaker Route." From Cincinnati, Ohio, it ran north to Toledo. From there it ran to Adrian and from there to Ypsilanti and Detroit. Another route known as the "Illinois Line" ran from Missouri to Chicago and Wisconsin. Other lines ran through Indiana to Cassopolis and Coldwater. More lines ran through Pennsylvania and New York.

When the escaping slaves reached Michigan they were taken to the villages that had developed along the Chicago Road and the Territorial Road. Many villages along these roads had stations on the Underground Railroad in them or in the nearby farming area. On reaching Michigan, the escaping slaves were taken eastward to Detroit or Port Huron. From these places they were taken across the border into Canada.

Although Michigan was a free state, under the Fugitive Slave Act of 1793, there was always a danger to the blacks living here that runaway slaves could be legally arrested by their masters, or agents, and taken back south. Free blacks also lived in constant fear of being kidnapped and forced into slavery, for at that time blacks had no legal standing in any court. A good example of this fear is found in the Crosswhite case that took place at Marshall, Michigan, in 1846.

Mr. Crosswhite, a mulatto fugitive slave, his wife and their five children were living in a little home in Marshall. All the Crosswhite family were well liked by their neighbors. The youngest child had been born in Michigan and under Michigan law was a free born child. Mr. Crosswhite's master came to Marshall looking for the family. About four o'clock one morning four men and the local sheriff went to Mr. Crosswhite's home to take the family back to Kentucky. When Mr. Crosswhite refused to open the door of his home the slavery men broke down the door. Friends came to Mr. Crosswhite's rescue and the slave catchers were arrested for breaking and entering. They were found guilty in a local court but later they won their case in a higher court. Friends of the Crosswhite family took the family to freedom in Canada.

Other cases like this one angered the southerners who were losing slaves because of the activities of the Underground Railroad. As a result, congress passed the Fugitive Slave Law of 1850. This act doubled the penalties of the law of 1793. This act angered many people and they joined the abolitionist movement. The law, in spite of its harshness, did not keep blacks from escaping to the North or stop the activities of the Underground Railroad. In fact it has been estimated that between 1850 and 1860 more than 5,000 slaves crossed the Detroit River to freedom in Canada. Because of its location more slaves entered Canada across the Detroit River than at any other place.

Battle Creek, because of the Quakers living there, became one of the major stations on the Underground Railroad. To this city came, in 1856, a tall, illiterate black woman who was an ex-slave from New York State. She took as her name Sojourner Truth. As she traveled about the country she told about the evils of slavery as she knew from having been a slave herself. Her activities did much to aid the anti-slavery movement in Michigan.

Escaping slaves brought nothing with them. They did not have warm enough clothing for the colder northern winters; but food and clothing were provided for them by members of the Underground Railroad and charitable organizations in the North and in Canada. Many slaves escaped on their own, hiding by day and walking north at night. It is hard to tell how many people gained their freedom this way.

Often ex-slaves did not have skills to work with northern crops and it was very difficult for them to make a living when they first arrived.

In 1863, a black regiment was formed in Michigan to fight on the side of the North during the Civil War. It was made up of black men from both Michigan and those who came back to Michigan from Canada. The men in this regiment were quartered in poorly constructed barracks on the east side of Detroit. Most of the men in this 102 United States Colored Infantry were men who had been born as slaves in slave states.

When the Civil War was over, many of the escaped slaves who had fled to Canada, as well as many from Michigan, returned to the South where the climate was warmer and they were more at home among other black people.

Questions to Check Your Reading

1. When were black slaves first brought to the United States?

2. What did the Ordinance of 1787 say about slavery?

3. Why was the Fugitive Slave Law of 1793 passed?

4. How did the cotton gin affect slavery?

5. Who founded the first anti-slavery society in Michigan?

6. What was the Underground Railroad? How was it operated?

7. What was the Crosswhite case? Where did it take place?

8. What factors made it difficult for escaped slaves to live in the North?

Things to Do

1. If you live in one of the cities along the Underground Railroad lines try to find out about the work of the Underground Railway in your area. Where were the stations located?

2. Use an encyclopedia or history book and find out about underground activities in other states — New York for example.

3. Listen to the cassette tape from the Aural Press series, **Remember the Ladies** about Sojourner Truth.

4. Locate some of the cities and villages that might have had underground stations in them.

5. What information can you find in your library about slavery in the South before the Civil War?

6. Look at a copy of the Ordinance of 1787 and the United States constitution and see what they say about returning slaves to their masters.

7. To learn about Michigan men in the Civil War listen to the tape "4th of July Moore" about our 25th infantry from **Voices from Michigan's Past.**

Kinchen Artis, a Quaker who came to Michigan from Ohio, was a corporal in Company K, First Michigan Colored Regiment. (Michigan State Archives)

Laura Haviland of Adrian was a leader of one of Michigan's most important anti-slavery groups. (Michigan State Archives)

This marker in Jackson shows where the Republican Party was founded in 1854. Many of its first members were anti-slavery. (Michigan State Archives)

Though best known for his defeat at Little Big Horn in 1876, Monroe resident George Armstrong Custer first gained fame as a 24-year-old general at the Battle of Gettysburg in 1863. (Custer Battlefield National Monument)

Chapter 8

The Iron and Copper Story

The Prehistoric Copper Miners

In an earlier chapter you read about how copper and iron ore formed in the old Killarney Mountains. Much of the copper formed in a pure state that needs no refining to be used. Today we know that this pure copper was used by a people who lived here long ago. On Isle Royale, the Keweenaw Peninsula, and other places around Lake Superior many pits have been found in the rocks from which a prehistoric people once took pure copper. The mining of this native copper was Michigan's oldest mining industry.

We know very little about these prehistoric miners, for few traces of their culture have been found. But we do know that they used fire to heat the rock boulders in the pits. Tests on ashes, from these early pit fires, show that these early miners worked in the pits about four thousand years ago by testing for the radioactive carbon which is left behind. When the rock mass had been heated, cold water was then poured onto it to cool it quickly and make a piece of rock break. The rock thus broken was then pounded with other rocks, called hammerstones, to shatter it and free the copper from the rock. Many broken hammerstones were left by the miners near the pits in which they had been working. Most of them have a groove around them so that a handle could be fastened to each one

by means of a leather thong. This gave the miners a stronger striking force.

The stone on the left is a barbed axe. The one on the right is a hammerstone used by prehistoric miners to mine copper ore. Note the groove to hold a handle and the broken lower end.

Though copper melts at a low temperature the prehistoric miners, because they had no bellows to force air into the fire, were not able to make a fire hot enough to melt copper. But by means of pounding the pieces of copper they hardened them and made spear points, arrowheads, knives, fish hooks, and some jewelry. Many of these copper artifacts have been found in burial mounds that have been opened.

When the Frenchmen came to the Lake Superior area the Indians living there had some small pieces of copper which they had found on the ground or along the shore. Sometimes they made these pieces of copper into jewelry, fish hooks or arrow points but they knew nothing about the copper pits or the earlier people who had long before them taken copper from the pits.

To Check How Well You Read

1. Where did the prehistoric people find copper?
2. How did they free the copper from the parent rock?
3. How did they use the copper? Why didn't they smelt it?
4. Where did the later Indians get their copper?

Things to Do

1. To learn more about mining read **The Cliff** by Chaput or **Old Reliable** by Lankton and Hyde.
2. Compare a piece of copper and iron. Try scratching both with something hard. Which is softer? Try a piece of lead too. To make copper, etc. harder, other materials are added which gives an alloy.

The Early Copper Mines

When Michigan became a state Douglass Houghton was appointed the first state geologist. In his report, in 1841, Houghton stated that both copper and iron ore had been found in the **western part** of the Upper Peninsula but that the deposits so far discovered were not large enough to be mined.

In 1842, the United States government made a treaty with the Chippewa Indians by which the Chippewa gave to the United States the last of their tribal lands in the Upper Peninsula. This treaty opened the area for prospectors to search for copper deposits. The reports of Douglass Houghton interested many people. In 1843, and for the next few years, many people came to the western part of the Upper Peninsula to look for copper deposits. Copper Harbor, Eagle Harbor, and Eagle River were busy places during the summer months when the prospectors set up their camps on the shore and then walked inland looking for a deposit of copper. Many mining claims were staked out and more than one hundred

Copper Harbor as seen from Brockway Mountain Drive. Copper Harbor is at the top of the Keweenaw Peninsula. Photo, 1966.

mining companies had been formed by 1846.

The first paying copper mine was the Cliff mine which had been started in Keweenaw County in 1844. Soon this mine was producing large amounts of pure copper. In 1848, the Minesota mine at Rockland, in Ontonagon County, was started. For many years it was also a large producer of copper. Michigan had become the leading copper producing state. Copper was discovered at Calumet in 1865. This copper deposit was one of the best. Mines were also opened in the Houghton-Hancock area.

Many communities in the Keweenaw Peninsula and the nearby area grew because of the copper mines. Some of these mining communities were Calumet, Laurium, Mass, Rockland, Hancock, Houghton, Painsdale, Phoenix, Delaware and Mohawk. The leading ports from which the copper was shipped were Eagle River, Eagle Harbor, Copper Harbor, Houghton, Hancock, and Ontonagon. All supplies for the miners had to be brought in by boat in the summer time. There were then no roads in the Upper Peninsula. Sometimes a man and a team of dogs would go through the forest to Green Bay,

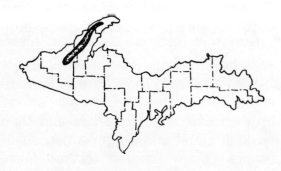

Copper deposits

Wisconsin, and get the mail for the copper and iron miners.

At first it was costly to portage the mining supplies around the rapids in the Saint Mary's River and to ship out the copper. When the "Soo" canal was opened, in 1855, it was easier to get supplies and cheaper to ship the copper by boat to the lower lakes. This was one of the main reasons for building the canal.

Although some copper was mined on Isle Royale, most of Michigan's copper has come from the Keweenaw Peninsula and in the area south of Ontonagon. Most of Michigan's copper is found in a pure state and is called native copper. Some of it formed in solid masses in the gas holes of the rock that filled the conduits of old volcanoes. Some of Michigan's best copper mines were dug into these ancient volcano conduits. Loose rocks and sand are often bound together by a bonding agent to form a rock known as a conglomerate. In some areas of the Keweenaw Peninsula; such as, at Calumet, Allouez and Copper City this bonding agent was pure copper. Such a copper and rock mixture is called conglomerate copper. Mines at these places worked that kind of copper deposit. At other places copper formed as mass sheets in the cracks and fissures of the rock mass. Such deposits were called mass copper. The Minesota mine worked this kind of deposit. Some very small pieces of pure copper were also deposited in the huge layer of Nonesuch shale that formed in the southern end of the copper range. It is from this Nonesuch shale that the White Pine mine now secures its copper.

How Well Did You Read?

1. Who was Michigan's first geologist?
2. What Indians ceded land to the United States government in the western part of the Upper Peninsula?
3. Which one was Michigan's first copper mine?
4. Why was it costly to ship supplies to the mines?
5. Where were the copper mines located?
6. In what four ways was copper found?
7. Name two of Michigan's copper mines.

Things to Do and Talk About

1. What are some of the uses for copper today?
2. If you have visited the Keweenaw Peninsula tell the class what you saw there.
3. Copper has two physical properties that make it very useful. Name them.

Map Work

Locate these places on your outline map: Cliff, Rockland, Calumet, Laurium, Mass, Eagle Harbor, Eagle River, Copper Harbor, Hancock, Houghton, Central and Ontonagon.

Michigan's Early Iron Mines

In 1844, William Burt, a government surveyor, and his party of surveyors were working on a survey line near the present city of Negaunee. As they worked they noticed that their compass was being drawn from its correct position by some unknown force. On looking around the area the surveyors found pieces of magnetic iron ore. Then they knew it was this magnetic iron ore that was making their compass act so strangely.

In 1845, the first Michigan iron ore mining company was organized in Jackson, Michigan. Two years later this company began mining iron ore at the Jackson mine not far from Negaunee. Because of the difficulty in shipping the iron ore in the small sailboats of the time, and the cost of portaging the iron ore around the Saint Mary's rapids, the company tried to smelt the ore near where it was mined. From the hardwood in the area charcoal was made. This was used to heat the iron ore in forges to make iron bars called blooms that could more easily be shipped. Soon other mines in the area west of Marquette were being worked and the area became known as the Marquette range.

The Marquette range starts near Marquette and runs westward for about twenty-two miles. In this range several mining centers developed. They were Negaunee, Ishpeming, Michigamme, Gwinn and Republic. The iron ore

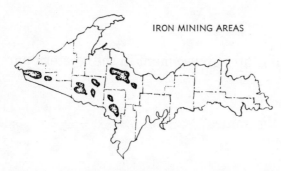

IRON MINING AREAS

mined on this range was sent to the ore docks at Marquette, on Lake Superior, or to Escanaba on Lake Michigan after a railroad was built to that port in the early 1860s.

To work the copper and iron mines Cornishmen from the copper mines in Cornwall, in England, came to northern Michigan. They brought with them much experience in copper mining. Later, Finns, Swedes, Irish and Italians came to the mining towns to find work in the copper and iron mines. Many French Canadians came to work in the woods to cut trees to make charcoal or huge timbers to be used as supports in the mines.

The Fayette Iron Furnace at Fayette on the Garden Peninsula. Charcoal was used to smelt the iron ore in the early furnaces like this one. Photo, 1965.

There were many difficulties that these early mining companies had to

overcome before iron mining became a paying industry. The iron ore had to be hauled from the mines to the lake port at Marquette. At first it was carried in wagons and sleighs. Later a strap iron railroad was built from Negaunee to the ore dock at Marquette. Horses and mules pulled small cars filled with iron ore along the steep tracks. Sometimes the ore cars ran too fast and killed the horses or mules. Later a railroad was built to haul the iron ore. Before the "Soo" locks were built, all the ore had to be unloaded from the boat and portaged around the rapids in the Saint Mary's River and then placed on other boats for shipment to ports on Lake Erie. In 1848, only three tons of iron were produced. In 1855, when the canal was opened, the amount had grown to 1,447 tons.

The second iron range, called the Menominee Range, was opened about 1875 when the Vulcan mine began production. The Menominee Range runs south and west of Marquette County into Iron and Dickinson counties. Here are found the iron mining communities of Vulcan, Iron Mountain, Crystal Falls, Iron River and Stambaugh. Most of the iron ore from this range was shipped to Escanaba.

The third iron range, called the Gogebic Range, was discovered in 1884. This range runs through the far western end of the Upper Peninsula and on into Wisconsin. Here are now found the former mining centers of Ironwood, Bessemer and Wakefield. The iron ore from this district was shipped to Ashland, Wisconsin.

To Check Your Reading

1. How did they happen to find iron ore?
2. What was the name of the first iron mining company?
3. How was the iron ore taken to Marquette?
4. How did the opening of the "Soo" Canal aid the iron mining industry?
5. What are the names of Michigan's three iron ranges?
6. Where did many early miners come from?

Things to Do and Talk About

1. Read **The Saga of Iron Mining in Michigan's Upper Peninsula** by Boyum to learn more about iron mining.
2. If someone in your area has samples of iron ore show them to the class.
3. How is steel made from iron?
4. In the past there have been gold mines in Michigan. Read about them in **Eberly's Michigan Journal** Sept.-Oct. issue, 1981.

Map Work

1. Find the following places on a map of Michigan: Negaunee, Ishpeming, Michigamme, Gwinn, Republic, Champion, Vulcan, Iron Mountain, Iron River, Crystal Falls, Stambaugh, Ironwood, Bessemer, and Wakefield.
2. Show where the Saint Mary's Falls Ship Canal is located in the St. Mary's River at Sault Ste. Marie, Michigan.

Working in the Early Copper and Iron Mines

Working in the early copper and iron mines was different than mining today where much machinery is used. During the early days of mining all of the work had to be done by men and horses or mules. As the men dug deeper and deeper into the rock of the mine, drill holes for the blasting charges had to be made by pounding on the end of an iron drill. Usually one man held the iron bar while two or three other men struck the upright end with heavy sledge hammers. Blasting was done by using gun powder. When the rock was shattered it was pounded with sledge hammers to reduce the size of the iron chunks or to free the copper from it. It then had to be shoveled into buckets. The buckets were then hauled to the surface by a team of horses that walked in a circle around a large wooden drum, called a horse whim, on which rope was wound. As the rope was wound around the drum the bucket of ore was raised from the mine.

Year after year the mines went

Eagle Harbor on the Keweenaw Peninsula. Early prospectors came here looking for copper deposits.

came into the mines. Better blasting powder was used. Machine powered drills were used to drill the holes for blasting. Huge steam hoists were used to turn the large drums on which steel cables were wound when a skip full of ore was raised from the mines. Crushers replaced men with sledge hammers to break up the rock. Telephone lines were later used in the mines so that those on the ground could talk to the men who were working deep underground. By 1896, one of the shafts at Calumet was 4,900 feet deep and at the Quincy mine, at Hancock, the shaft was also nearing the 5,000 foot level below ground.

deeper and deeper into the rock of the Killarney Mountains. At first these mines were dark, damp places in which to work. The only light the miners had was a candle placed on the brim of their caps. Later these candles were replaced by acetylene lamps that gave a bright light. Each miner wore one of these carbide lights on the front of his cap. Later electric lights were used in the iron and copper mines. As the mines went deeper and deeper into the ground huge pumps were used to keep the water pumped out of the mines. Some mines pumped enough water each day to supply a good sized city. Fresh air had to be blown into the mines. This required more expensive machinery.

As the years passed other changes

Cornish pump at Iron Mountain. Huge pumps like these were used to pump the water out of the copper and iron mines. Photo, 1959.

How Carefully Did You Read?

1. How were the holes first made for the blasting powder?
2. How were the large pieces of copper and iron ore reduced in size?
3. How was the copper and iron raised from the mines?
4. What did the early miners use for light? What later lights were used?
5. How was the water kept out of the mines?
6. What were some of the later changes in mining?
7. How deep into the ground did some of the copper mines go?

Things to Do and Talk About

1. What was a horse whim and how did it work?
2. How did telephones aid the miners?
3. Does it get hotter or colder the deeper a mine goes?

The Decline of the Copper Mines

Between 1850 and 1900 many copper mines were started in the old Killarney Mountains. Many lasted only a short time while others produced for years and paid their owners huge profits. During these years Michigan was a leading copper producing state. Her peak year of copper production was in 1916 when 136,846 tons of copper were produced. Since that time copper production has declined. As the cost of mining copper increased, because of the depth of the shafts, it became difficult to compete against the new open pit copper mines in Arizona, Utah and Montana. When profits dropped, many of the mines were abandoned and allowed to fill with water. As the mines closed many miners moved away and found employment elsewhere, especially in the growing cities of southeastern Michigan where new industries were developing after 1900.

The Phoenix Mine dump. As one drives through the copper and iron mining area one often sees these remains of earlier mining activity.

Today, water-filled shafts, rusting machinery, piles of waste rock, and a few weathered buildings are all that remain in many places to remind one of the busy days when miners, with pick and shovel and blasting powder, once mined copper from the rock almost a mile below the land on which their houses sat and their children played. Some of the mining communities still remain but in many of them there is less activity than there was during the busy mining days. Many of the mining communities like Cliff, Allouez, Phoenix and Delaware have completely disappeared and are now known as ghost towns. Often only a pile of waste rock or a sign marks the location of what was once a busy mining community.

In 1969, the few remaining copper mines north of Hancock ceased operating. Since that time Michigan's only remaining copper mine has been the White Pine mine which is located on M64 between Lake Gogebic and Lake Superior. Here very small pieces of copper and copper sulphide along with a small amount of silver are taken from the Nonesuch shale that underlies the area. The shale is ground to a fine powder. Then the unwanted shale is removed by a flotation process which leaves the small pieces of copper. These are then melted and the molten copper is then poured into molds to form copper bars.

Much copper still remains in the abandoned copper mines but the cost of mining it became too expensive to keep the mines in operation. However, new exploration work was started at the Centennial mine, near Calumet, to find out if enough copper remains to make mining pay a profit. Other exploration work is also being done in other areas too.

To Check Your Reading

1. What year was Michigan's peak year in copper production?

2. What is a ghost town?

3. What is the name of Michigan's only copper mine today? Where is it located?

4. How does this mine get its copper?

Things to Do and Talk About

1. Find out which states are the leading copper producers today. How much copper do they produce?

2. From what countries does the United States get copper?

3. Listen to the cassette tape about the 1913 copper strike from the series, **Voices From Michigan's Past.**

Getting Iron Ore Today

So vast has been the mining of iron ore in Michigan and Minnesota, during the last hundred years, that nearly all of the natural high grade ore in the Lake Superior area has been mined and shipped away.

Only four iron mines are open in Michigan today. These are all open pit mines. All of the deep shaft mines have closed.

It is possible that this will change in the future as the need for iron increases or decreases.

As the reserves of iron ore in the Lake Superior area grew smaller the steel companies began looking for iron ore deposits in other countries. They also became interested in new methods to use the low grade ores. Large de-

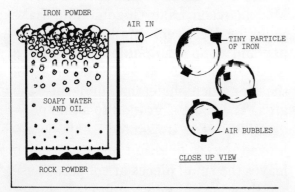

FLOTATION PROCESS . . . REMOVES ROCK POWDER FROM ORE

IRON POWDER
AIR IN
TINY PARTICLE OF IRON
SOAPY WATER AND OIL
AIR BUBBLES
CLOSE UP VIEW
ROCK POWDER

The flotation process is like a bubble bath. Air is blown through a soapy mixture of crushed crude ore, oil and water. The iron and rock separate because the iron sticks to the oil film on the bubbles.

posits of high grade ore have been located in several countries. One of these deposits was located in Canada northeast of the city of Quebec. Large mines and taconite plants have been opened in this area, some 360 miles north of the port of Sept-Iles on the Saint Lawrence River. At Sept-Iles huge ore docks have been built. To these docks, and to others on the Saint Lawrence River, huge new ore carriers, large enough to carry one hundred thousand tons of iron ore, come to carry the iron ore to ocean ports throughout the world. Smaller lake boats bring the ore up the St. Lawrence waterway to receiving ports along the southern shore of Lake Erie. Some iron ore is also shipped to the United States from other countries.

Much iron ore of a lower concentration, called taconite in Minnesota and jasper in Michigan, remains in the Lake Superior area. New processes, known as beneficiation, now make it possible to crush these lower grades of sedimentary rock and make high concentrates of iron ore from them. First the hard mother lode containing the iron ore that was deposited on the ocean floor

The Sherwood Mine at Iron River. Photo, 1956.

during the Huronian Period long before the Killarney Mountains were formed, has to be blasted from its hard rock layer. It is then taken and crushed. Then the rock is ground in ball mills until it is a fine powder. In Minnesota, where the ore is magnetic, the iron can be taken from this powder by a magnet, but in Michigan, where most of the ore is not magnetic, the iron ore is taken from the powder by a flotation process.

When the iron ore has been taken from the mother lode in this manner, it is then processed into small pellets about the size of walnuts. The pellets are then heated and dried until they are hard. Most of the taconite from the Lake Superior area comes from Minnesota where huge concentrating plants have been built but some of the pellets come from Michigan. New taconite plants have been built at the Humboldt mine and the Republic mine which are in Marquette County where the ore is best for processing. One other mine, the Hanna mine, is located on the Menominee Range.

To get iron ore by means of the new concentration processes is a very expensive way but in the development of these new processes lies the future of the iron mining areas of the Upper Peninsula and the Lake Superior region. Much of the iron ore coming down the lakes today is in the form of these man made concentrates. They are much preferred by the furnace men over the older natural ores as they melt more evenly in the furnaces and the furnaces can increase their production from twenty-five to one hundred percent and thus save money in the smelting process.

To Check Your Reading

1. What has happened to most of the high grade ore in the Lake Superior region?
2. How is the low grade ore now being used to make taconite pellets?

Things to Do and Talk About

1. Find Sept-Iles on a map of eastern Canada.
2. Why is less iron ore now passing through the "Soo" canal?
3. Taconite processing has been in the news because it leaves large amounts of waste called tailings. Find out about this and why some people are upset.

4. Explain the difference between open pit and shaft mining.
5. Look in the **Atlas of Michigan** to learn more about mineral deposits in our state.

Top: Breaking up pieces of ore by hand at Negaunee, Michigan in 1863. (Michigan State Archives, History Division)
Bottom: Miners drilling holes for explosives in an iron ore mine, 1960. (Gogebic Industrial Bureau)

Chapter 9

Michigan's Forests of Yesterday and Today

A Forest Land

Up to one hundred and fifty years ago, when settlers began clearing land to make farms, almost all of Michigan was covered with trees. Because of the different kinds of soil that had developed, the amount of rainfall, and the differences in land drainage and sunshine, many kinds of trees grew in Michigan. These forest areas can be grouped into three general types.

One type of forest was known as a hardwood forest. Hardwood trees grew in the southern half of the Lower Peninsula, in some areas in the upper part of the Lower Peninsula, and in the western part of the Upper Peninsula. These hardwood forests grew where better soils had developed. In these hardwood forest areas grew maple, beech, elm, ash, hickory, walnut and oak trees. These trees have broad leaves and are known as deciduous trees because they shed their leaves each fall. At first these trees were cut and burned as the settlers cleared land in the southern part of the state, but as they became scarce, and more powerful saws were developed, these trees became valuable for their lumber.

A second type of forest was known as a softwood forest. In these forests grew Michigan's three kinds of pine trees with their green needles. They were the white pine, the Norway or red pine, and the jack pine. These pine trees grew on the poorer sandy soil north of a line from Bay City to Muskegon in the upper part of the Lower Peninsula and in the eastern part of the Upper Peninsula east of a line from Escanaba to Munising.

The white pine was the tree most wanted by the lumber industry between 1860 and 1900. You can easily learn to identify a white pine because there are five needles in each sheath and you can remember this because there are five letters in the word white.

Upon the poorer sandy soil grew the red pine, or as it was called the Norway pine. Red pines were the most common of Michigan's three pine trees. They can easily be identified by their reddish bark and the two long needles in each sheath. When one of the needles is bent it will break with a snap.

On the poorest sandy soil grew the jack pines. They can be identified by their two short needles. These trees were of little value to the lumbermen.

The third type of forest was known as the swamp forest. These were found in the low wet areas of the state such as in swampy areas and along streams. In these forests could be found such trees as birch, cedar, hemlock, spruce, tamarack, and balsam. Most of these trees were of little value to the lumbermen.

Michigan's forests were of no value before 1825 as there was no way to transport the heavy lumber to market. The opening of the Erie Canal made it possible to ship lumber all the way to New York City. As the lumber supply in the East declined, more and more lumber, to build the rapidly growing cities, began to be shipped to the East from the Great Lakes states. New railroads, spreading west across the plains, after the Civil War were soon carrying lumber from Milwaukee, Wisconsin, and Chicago, Illinois, to build the towns, cities, and farm buildings that were being built in the growing West. Much of this lumber came from Michigan's forests.

Reading Checks

1. Why do many kinds of trees grow in Michigan?
2. What kinds of trees grew in the hardwood forests? in the softwood forests? in the swamp forests?
3. How can you identify a white pine? a Norway pine? a jack pine?
4. How did the Erie Canal and the railroads aid the lumber industry?

Things to Do

1. What kinds of trees grow near your home? Learn what they are called and how to identify them. Use **Michigan Trees Worth Knowing** by Norman Smith.
2. Find out why the lumbermen wanted white pine trees for lumber.
3. Draw leaf outlines on cards and use them as flash cards to learn the tree names that go with them. Put the names on the back.

Nearly all of the cities and villages in the upper part of the Lower Peninsula and the eastern part of the Upper Peninsula had their beginning in the lumber industry. As the demand for lumber increased, as the pine forests in the East were cut, lumbermen began coming to Michigan searching for good stands of pine trees that could be cut to make lumber. Timber cruisers searched through the forests for the best stands of pine, along a river bank, where it could be cut and floated to mills at the river's mouth. When a good stand, called a pinery, had been found, the land was purchased from the government by some lumberman or lumber company.

At the mouths of the rivers along the shore of the Great Lakes small sawmills were built to cut the logs into lumber. In 1834, a sawmill was set up at Saginaw. By 1854, there were 61 sawmills in the state and by 1872 the number had grown to over 1,500.

Early in the fall a few men went into the forest to the place where the trees were to be cut and began putting up buildings for a lumber camp and getting ready for the men who would come

Lumberman's Memorial on the Au Sable River west of Oscoda. Inscription reads: Erected to perpetuate the memory of the pioneer lumbermen of Michigan through whose labors was made possible the development of the prairie states.

to cut the trees during the following winter. When winter came, men known as "lumberjacks" arrived to live at the camp and cut down the trees.

After about 1860 lumber camps were temporary buildings made from boards. After the trees were cut in one area the buildings were taken down and the lumber was then used again to make another lumber camp at some other place in the woods. One building housed the horses and oxen that were used to drag the logs from the woods to the river bank or to a railroad. Another smaller building served as a blacksmith shop. Here horses were kept sharp shod so that they would not slip on the icy roads. The blacksmith also repaired chains, made the sleigh runners, and did the other necessary iron

work that was needed in a logging camp. The men slept in another building known as the bunkhouse. Bunks for the men ran along the two sides of the narrow building. At first the bunkhouses were heated by an open fire in the center of the building but when stoves began to be made, large stoves that burned four foot wood were used to heat the bunkhouses. A stove pipe came up from the stove in the center of the bunkhouse. From there a stove pipe ran to each end of the bunkhouse and thus some heat was carried to the ends of the building. At night all wet clothing was hung on a wire, which ran parallel to the smoke stack, to dry. The men all washed in basins placed on a shelf at one end of the bunkhouse. Another building served as a cook house and dining room for the men. Here the hardy lumberjacks were served a hearty breakfast and supper. During the meals no one was allowed to talk. The noon meal was taken to the place where the men were working in the woods.

Another building served as a bunkhouse for the camp foreman, the bookkeeper, and sometimes the man who scaled the logs to find out how many board feet the men were cutting. In this building was also what was called the "van" which was a small store where such things as tobacco, mittens, socks, and other items were sold to the men working in the camp.

In the morning the lumberjacks ate a large breakfast. Then the teamsters harnessed their horses, or oxen, while others shouldered their axes and crosscut saws and then all started into the woods to do another day's work.

When a tree was chosen for sawlogs,

two men chopped it part way through with their axes. Then two other men using a crosscut saw started to saw through it from the opposite side. As the large teeth of the saw cut deeper into the tree's trunk the tree began to lean toward the chopped side. At last, with a mighty crash, the tree came down, breaking off part of its branches and some of those on nearby trees. When the tree was down, other men called limbers, chopped off all the branches. When the limbs were removed two other men, called buckers, cut the tree into sawlogs twelve, fourteen, sixteen or eighteen feet in length. Other woodsmen called "swampers" cleared a path through the tree tops and brush so that the logs could be dragged from the woods by teams of horses, or oxen. From the cutting area the logs were hauled to a rollway, on a river bank, or to a decking ground beside a railroad spur, on large bob-sleighs.

All winter long the lumberjacks worked, amid the snow and cold in the silent forest, cutting logs and hauling them to the river's edge. There the logs were piled in large piles at a place called a rollway. There each log was marked on its end with the owner's brand, or log mark, so that it could be sorted from the other logs, belonging to other lumbermen, at the end of the river drive. The brand was put into the end of each log by means of hitting the end of the log with a large hammer on the face of which the company mark was raised. When the hammer hit the log the imprint of the hammer left its mark in the end of the log.

At first all the pine logs were floated to the sawmills on the rivers. When the melting snows of spring had raised the water level in the rivers the logs were rolled from the river bank into the water and started on their way to the sawmills at the mouths of the rivers.

Some of the lumberjacks, called "riverjacks" or "white water men" kept the logs moving down stream. Sometimes they walked along the river bank and watched the logs as they floated on the river. At other times they rode the logs as they drifted along on the surface of the river. By late spring the lumberjacks were back from their winter in the woods. In the booms, at the river mouths, floated their winter's cut ready to be sawed into lumber in the sawmills that stood on the river bank.

Around these early sawmills communities developed with houses, churches, hotels, saloons, and stores. Michigan's lake port towns like Bay City, Saginaw, Alpena, Cheboygan, Muskegon and Manistee had come into being.

In the early lumbering days these sawmill towns were rough, rowdy places. All the supplies for each town, and the lumber camps up river, had to be brought there during the summer months by the sailboats that came to carry away the lumber, for there were then few roads and no railroads in the upper part of the Lower Peninsula or in the Upper Peninsula. As the cutting continued in the forests up the rivers, more buildings built with the lumber coming from the busy sawmills were built and the port villages grew in size as more homes and businesses were placed on the village lots. Some men, who just a few years before had worn the heavy, calked boots of a lumberjack, became wealthy and built large frame homes along the streets of the growing lumber towns. Some of these large homes, built of choice lumber, are still standing and to some people they are reminders of the days when pine was king and Michigan was a leading lumber producer.

At the lake ports, along the shores of Lake Huron and Lake Michigan, the newly cut lumber was carefully put into piles beside the docks to dry before being sent to market. The wind from the forest carried the pleasant pine smell high to keep the boats from entering. Into these harbors, during the warm weather shipping season, came the white-winged sailing schooners that had been built for carrying the lumber to market. Into their empty holds and upon their decks the lumber was piled. Then with sails spread to catch the offshore winds they started off across the lake. Soon even the tips of their sails had disappeared beyond the distant horizon. Another boat load of Michigan lumber had gone to market.

This is a nice view of what a river full of logs looks like. This log jam was caused by the flood of 1883 which destroyed several railway bridges in Grand Rapids, but the Michigan-Southern railroad bridge held back this large body of logs from running away until the water lowered, when many of them did go under the bridge.

of the drying lumber out over the lake and across the countryside.

The river mouths, especially on the western side of the state, made good harbors if the sand bars were not too Later much of the lumber was carried by the newer and faster steamboats that took the place of the older and slower sailing boats.

Reading Checks

1. What did timber cruisers do?
2. Who were the lumberjacks and what did they do?
3. What was a rollway?
4. How could a lumberman tell his logs from those of the logs belonging to another lumber company?
5. What was a bunkhouse? Describe one.
6. Why were the early sawmills located at the mouths of the rivers?
7. List five lumber jobs and the names that go with them.
8. How was the lumber taken to market?

Things to Do and Talk About

1. Is there anyone in your area who can tell your class about the lumbering days?
2. Why was most of the lumbering work done in the winter? What did the lumberjacks do the rest of the year?
3. Here are some books to read about this era: **The Wooden River,** by Nancy Stone and **Daylight in the Swamp** by Robert W. Wells. You may want to listen to the cassette tape on the White Pine Era from the **Voices from Michigan's Past** series.
   There is a fine filmstrip about 19th century lumbering called **Logging in Michigan.** It is available from Hillsdale Educational Publishers.

Map Work

1. Look on the map with the rivers of Michigan on it and try to figure out which ones were logging rivers. What logging towns are on these rivers?

Changes in the Lumber Industry

As the lumbermen cut farther and farther back into the forests away from the streams, the team haul to a rollway on a river bank became longer and longer. This greatly increased the cost of producing saw logs. In order to reduce expenses and also to harvest the trees that stood between the rivers, lumbermen began building privately owned spur railroads that connected with the new railroad lines then being built in the upper part of the state. At first the railroads often hauled the logs to one of the old rollways but before long they were hauling the logs all the way to the sawmills and the river drives became fewer and fewer. The last river drive was on the Menominee River in 1910. When an area had been cut the rails were taken up and used to make a new spur line into a new cutting area. Many miles of these old abandoned logging railroad grades can still be traced in Michigan's forest areas. Railroads also changed logging operations in two other ways. By using railroads, saw logs could be brought to the mills all year long. Sawmills then began running in

This is the way a sawmill would have looked in the 1870's-90's. The log and the men are on a platform that moves on rails while the saw stands still.

These big wheels were an invention that allowed logs to be moved all year long. The logs were chained to the axle under the wheels and dragged by the horses.

Both pictures are courtesy of the Clark Historical Library. Central Michigan University.

the winter as well as in the summer. As the pine trees grew less and less in number, more and more hardwood trees were used to make lumber. This was made possible by the better saws, now driven by steam power, and the fact that the railroads could haul the hardwood trees, that usually did not float on water, to the sawmills.

Loading pine logs on a flatcar at Deward, northwest of Frederic, in 1903. (Photo courtesy of Ace Leng.)

As the cutting continued, the cost of hauling the saw logs to the older port sawmill towns became too expensive. It was cheaper to haul them to the new, growing inland towns such as Cadillac, Grayling, Deward, Seney, and Lewiston, and then ship the lumber to market by railroad. These new sawmill towns came into being on rivers where a railroad crossed and on inland lakes where the logs could be floated in booms near the mills. Several of these inland sawmill towns sprang up in the upper part of the Lower Peninsula and in the eastern part of the Upper Peninsula between 1875 and 1900.

Between 1870 and 1900 one third of the state was lumbered and Michigan led the states in the amount of lumber produced. During the years that Michigan was a leading lumber producing state many changes were made in the lumber industry. At first the trees were cut only in the wintertime but after 1880 large wheels were made so it was possible to bring the saw logs from the woods in the summertime. The logs were chained to the axle and rolled away.

During the pioneer days much of the lumber was sawed by hand with a saw called a pit saw. One man, called the sawyer, stood on the log and pulled the saw blade upward. Another man, called the pitman, stood in the pit under the saw and pulled the blade downward to make the cut. Sometimes little water powered sawmills were built to cut the logs into lumber. In these mills a pit saw was held upright in a wooden frame called a gate. It was called a gate saw. A gate saw was slow and cut lumber about as fast as it could be cut by men using a pit saw. Later a similar saw, without the heavy wooden frame, and known as a muley saw, increased the rate of cutting. The muley saw was followed by the circular saw and that by the band saw that cut a smaller slot and thus saved much lumber.

Checking Your Reading

1. Why did the lumbermen build railroads to carry their logs to the sawmills?
2. On what river was Michigan's last river drive? Find this river, in the western part of the Upper Peninsula, on your map of Michigan.
3. In what ways did railroads change the logging industry?

4. How did big wheels affect logging?

5. Why did the hardwoods become more valuable?

Things to Do

1. Can you find pictures of the various kinds of saws that were used?

2. If you live in a former sawmill town try to find out about the area during the lumbering days.

3. Use Eric Sloane's book, **A Reverence for Wood,** to learn why some kinds of wood are better suited for certain uses.

A Waste Land

When the lumberjacks had cut the trees and gone on to new cuttings they left behind many stumps, dried branches, and rotting bark. These cut-over areas were called "slashings." During the summer, when the land was dry, this debris, left by the lumbermen, often caught on fire. Because there was no way to check these fires they often

Pine stumps on the Kingston Plains, near Seney, show that once pine trees grew in this area. Today new tree plantings are once again making northern Michigan a forest land. Photo, 1967.

burned over large areas before they were finally stopped by rains. At night the sky was crimson because of the flames and by day the sun was seen as an orange ball because of the smoke and soot that filled the air. Sometimes these fires destroyed not only the slash-

ings but also many villages and, as in the great fires of 1871 and 1881, took many lives as well because people could not escape from the rapidly advancing flames.

Much of the upper part of the Lower Peninsula, and the eastern part of the Upper Peninsula, was burned by these forest fires. In some areas the fires burned over the slashings several times. When these fires had passed there remained behind only a black burned over area of charred logs, stumps and dusty ash that covered the ground. Often nothing green remained as far as one could see. So hot were these fires that they not only burned the debris upon the ground but also the best ground, called humus, itself.

When the fires had passed, a new force called erosion then set to work to further destroy the cut-over land. The forests had kept the soil in place but now that they were gone, the soil that remained began to blow away as the winds passed across the cut-over lands. This work of erosion was further increased by the sudden rains of summer that dropped water on the land faster than it could be absorbed. As the water ran away it carried some of the soil. So completely was much of this soil destroyed that it will be many years before some areas will again have soil deep enough to grow trees of any size.

As the lumberjacks went on to new cutting areas many of the little sawmill towns, that for a brief time had been busy sawmill centers, declined in size or were completely abandoned and became what are now known as "ghost towns." The sawmills ran less and less, as fewer and fewer logs came from the forest, until they stopped altogether. In some of these sawmill towns the mills caught on fire and were burned. In others the mills were wrecked for their lumber, which with the machinery, was sent to a new area to make new sawmills nearer to where logs were being cut in the forest. The yellow sawdust piles that once stood beside the mills turned to a gray-rotting wood. The sawdust covered streets, where once horses had hauled wagons, soon were filled with grass and weeds. Board sidewalks, on which busy people had once gone about the tasks of their day, lay rotting in the tall grass that grew between the boards. Many houses in the sawmill towns were wrecked for their lumber.

Others stood for years with broken windows, sagging roofs, and doors that swung noisily on creaking hinges as the winds from the cut-over lands passed unhindered through buildings that had once been homes and business places.

After the lumbermen had cut the trees from the land they no longer had any use for it. Sometimes some of the men who had worked in the lumber camps, bought pieces of the cut-over land from the lumber companies and started farms in the area. But the soil, except in a few scattered areas, was very poor and the climate too cool for producing most crops. For a few years these little farms were worked but many of them have been abandoned. Most of the land was abandoned by the lumber companies and when they stopped paying taxes it was again claimed by the state. Thousands of acres of this abandoned land, along with hundreds of deserted farms, now belong to the state of Michigan. Much of it is now state or national forest land where new green forests are replacing the burned-over land.

How Well Did You Read?

1. What became of many of the sawmill towns?

2. What were slashings?

3. What were the forest fires like?

4. What is humus? erosion?

5. Why were many of the farms in this area abandoned?

6. Why did the lumbermen stop paying taxes on the land?

Problems and Things to Talk About

1. What is humus and why is it important to plant growth? What is a compost heap?
2. How can forest fires be prevented?
3. How do forest fires affect you where ever you live?
4. What can you find in your library about Michigan's forest fires?
5. Look in the series of books **Michigan Ghost Towns,** by R. L. Dodge — see if there are any near you.

The Department of Natural Resources and Its Work

Today, of the vast forests that once covered Michigan, very little is left. Only eighty acres of original pine and some of hardwood are left in the Lower Peninsula. Some original forest land still is found in the western part of the Upper Peninsula in the Huron Mountains and the Porcupine Mountains.

There came a time when people began to realize that Michigan's lumber harvest was fast coming to an end. If Michigan was to again be a producer of lumber, the state would have to help replant and then protect the forest areas. In 1921, the state Department of Conservation was set up to help Michigan save and better use her natural resources. This department is now called the Department of Natural Resources.

Today, this department is helping the people of Michigan to better understand the need for conserving and using our natural resources. It prints a magazine for those interested in the work of the department, loans motion pictures to schools and clubs, sends out people to talk to groups, and loans display exhibits showing wild animals. Part of its work is to establish state parks and care for them. There are now about seventy-five state parks in Michigan where people can camp, fish, swim, and enjoy the lakes, streams, and woods.

Another task of the Department of Natural Resources is to protect Michigan's forests from fires. Although there have been few large forest fires for several years, each year some damage is done to Michigan's forests and animal life by forest fires. Careless campers and smokers often cause the starting of forest fires. Other fires are started by glass from broken bottles that have been carelessly tossed away. Such broken glass often concentrates the sun's rays and this starts a fire if the area is dry. Sometimes lightning starts a fire. But most forest fires are man made. In the spring before the new vegetation has developed, in the summer when the land is hot and dry, and in the fall when the leaves have fallen, are the times when most of the forest fires are started.

For many years high metal towers, called fire towers, located on top of hills, were used by men to locate beginning forest fires. During dry periods men climbed to the top of these towers and spent hours there watching the area to spot any fire starting. Today, men in airplanes can cover a much larger area at much less expense. Once a fire has been spotted, they can fly close to it and report its location. Then fire-fighting equipment is sent to put out the fire.

The department also maintains nurseries where seeds are planted and little trees for replanting are grown. Some seedlings are sold to be used to control erosion, provide cover for wildlife or to make windbreaks. Many seedlings are planted on state forest lands each year.

The national government has four national forests in Michigan. The Ottawa and Hiawatha national forests are in the Upper Peninsula. The Manistee and Huron national forests are in the upper part of the Lower Peninsula. To produce pine seedlings for these forests the national government has two nurseries in Michigan. One is called the J. W. Toumey Tree Nursery and is located near Watersmeet in the Upper Peninsula. The other is the Chittenden Nursery at Wellston, near Manistee in the Lower Peninsula.

Besides these state and national forests, several people have tree farms where Christmas trees and other trees are grown. Each year Michigan markets thousands of Christmas trees. In other vast areas of the once burned-over land trees have been planted or have reseeded themselves. As one drives through the area today one again sees second growth trees now covering much of the area.

Pine seedlings. Chittenden nursery near Wellston.

To Check Your Reading

1. What is the Department of Natural Resources?

2. What are some of the things that the Department of Natural Resources does?

3. Why does the state have tree nurseries? Where are they located?

4. How are forest fires controlled?

5. What are the names of the four national forests in Michigan?

Problems and Things to Do

1. Some maps show the state and national forests of Michigan. Use the book **Michigan County Maps and Recreation Guide** by the Michigan Conservation Clubs.

2. Look at the **Michigan Mapskills and Information** book or on a state highway map and learn the types of facilities that are available in state parks near you.

3. Find out how much it costs to visit or camp in state and national parks in Michigan.

Top: Lumbermen from the old days. (Clarke Historical Library, Central Michigan University)
Bottom: The Ford lumber operation at Iron Mountain in 1948. How do the logs get from the flat cars to the chute? (Ford News Bureau)

Chapter 10

Water Transportation

The Great Lakes and the St. Lawrence Waterway

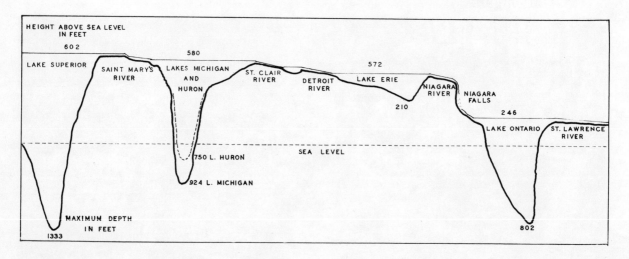

The Great Lakes that lie on, or near, Michigan's boundary are the largest group of fresh water lakes in the world. Hundreds of streams flow into the Great Lakes. These streams and the Great Lakes form the headwaters of the St. Lawrence River drainage system.

Today, this lake and river system forms one of North America's main waterway transportation routes but for many years, after the French settled at Quebec, shipping by way of this waterway was hindered by several natural obstacles. Between Montreal and Lake Ontario there were several rapids in the St. Lawrence River. A high waterfalls, known as Niagara Falls, was in the Niagara River between Lake Ontario and Lake Erie. Another rapids

was in the Saint Mary's River at Sault Ste. Marie. (Pronounced - Soo Saint Marie)

Because of these obstacles all freight was carried in canoes, and portaged when necessary, up to about 1800. But during the past one hundred and eighty years a series of canals and locks have been built, enlarged and deepened at different times, so that now the entire lake and river system is navigable for ships that do not sink more than twenty-seven feet into the water. The present canal, locks, river and lake system up the St. Lawrence River to Lake Ontario is known as the Saint Lawrence Seaway. It was opened to boat traffic in April 1959. To make it possible for boats to come and go from Lake Superior to the Atlantic Ocean several canals and locks had to be built and in other places the bottom of the waterway had to be deepened. The canals and locks in the St. Lawrence River above Montreal allow large boats to reach Lake Ontario. Another canal and series of locks, known as the Welland Canal, make it possible for boats to pass Niagara Falls and go between Lake Ontario and Lake Erie.

The following table will show you how the Great Lakes compare with the other large bodies of fresh water in the world:

Lake	Continent	Sq. Miles
Superior	North America	31,200
Victoria Nyanza	Africa	27,000
Huron	North America	23,000
Michigan	North America	22,450
Baikal	Asia	13,000
Tanganyika	Africa	12,500
Great Slave	North America	12,000
Great Bear	North America	11,500
Nyassa	Africa	11,000
Chad	Africa	10,000
Erie	North America	9,960
Winnipeg	North America	9,000
Ontario	North America	7,240

At the mouth of the Detroit River, just north of Lake Erie, a large channel called the Livingstone Channel, has been blasted into the Devonian limestone layer to deepen the river so that ships can pass up and down the river. Because Lake St. Clair is very shallow, a trench has been dredged across it to make the water deep enough for boats to cross the lake. Extensive dredging has also been done across the "flats" at the mouth of the Saint Clair River to straighten the channel in the St. Clair River at its mouth. Other channel work has been done at the Neebish cut in the Saint Mary's River.

Because Lake Huron and Lake Michigan have the same water level, ships can easily pass from one lake to the other through the Straits of Mackinac. In order for boats to pass the rapids in the Saint Mary's River and go between Lake Huron and Lake Superior another system of locks was built. This lock system known as the Saint Mary's Falls Ship Canal is commonly called the "Soo." From early spring, when the winter ice is broken, until late in December, when freezing weather and winter storms make the lakes too dangerous, lake freighters and foreign ships pass along this waterway carrying grain, coal, limestone, cement, iron ore, and manufactured products.

To Check What You Have Read

1. What is unusual about the five Great Lakes?
2. The Great Lakes are a part of what large river system?
3. Why were canoes the main means of transportation before 1800?
4. In what river is Niagara Falls? From what lake does the Niagara River flow? Into what lake does it empty? What canal now makes it possible for boats to pass between these two lakes?
5. Where is the Livingstone Channel located?
6. Why was it necessary to dredge a trench across Lake St. Clair?
7. How do boats go from Lake Huron to Lake Michigan?
8. What river flows out of Lake Superior? What rapids are in this river? What canal allows boats to go between Lake Huron and Lake Superior?

9. What size boats can use the St. Lawrence Waterway? Why is this important to ship builders and owners?

10. Which of the two Great Lakes have the same water level?

Things You Can Do and Talk About

1. Why are the Great Lakes filled with fresh water? How are these lakes now being polluted?

2. Look at Jacques Lesstrang's book, **Seaway,** to learn more about this important water system.

3. See if you can find out the last days ships can go through the seaway in the fall. Some people think it would be a good idea to keep the Lakes open for ships all year. What advantages and disadvantages would this idea have?

4. You may get some interesting ideas by reading **Fate of the Lakes,** by James Barry.

Map Work

1. On the outline map show the following: Montreal, St. Lawrence River, Lake Ontario, Niagara River, Lake Erie, Detroit River, Lake St. Clair, St. Clair River, Lake Huron, Georgian Bay, Straits of Mackinac, Lake Michigan, St. Mary's River and Lake Superior.

Early Shipping on the Great Lakes and Connecting Waters

During the French period, as you have learned, the canoe was the best means of water transportation. When the English became the masters of the Great Lakes, canoe transportation on the lakes declined as some sailboats began to be built. As yet the area was unsettled and furs and trade goods were still the main articles carried. After 1800, when settlers began coming to the Great Lakes area, major changes in transportation began to be made on the Great Lakes.

With the opening of the Erie Canal the upper Great Lakes became important highways of commerce and canoes were no longer sufficient to carry the settlers westward and their products back to the markets in the East. Sailboats and steamboats, that could cross the lakes, and carry a much larger cargo, began to be built for the carrying trade.

Boat building in the Great Lakes area became an important industry as the lake region supplied the needed material for building boats. White oak was used for the keel, ribs, and sides of the boats while tall straight pine or cedar were used for the masts to hold the sails. Many sailboats were built in the forests, along the bank of a stream. Men went into the woods and cut trees and then sawed them into lumber by using a pit saw. The newly cut lumber was then left to dry in the sunshine.

St. Lawrence Seaway and Great Lakes Ports

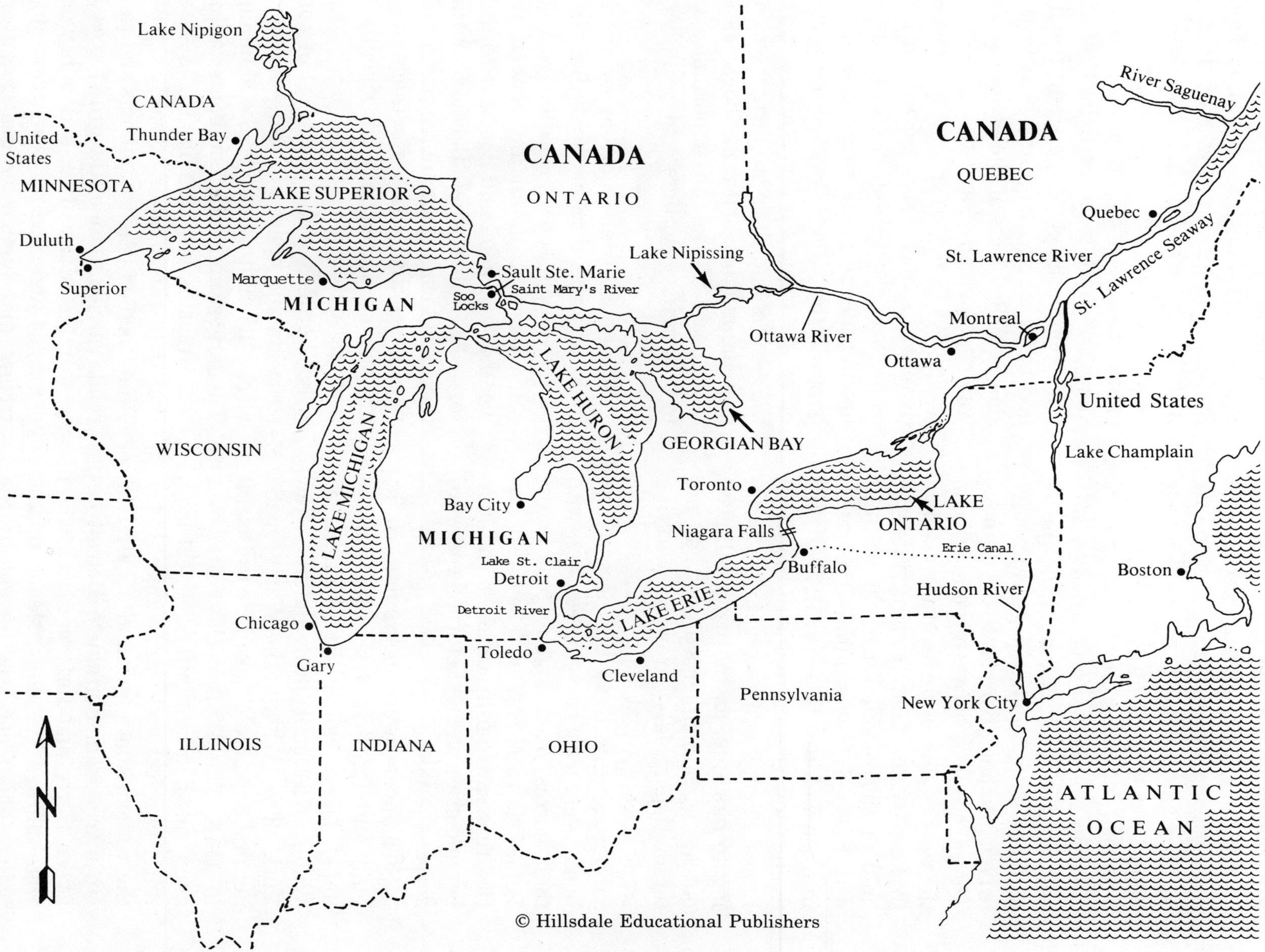

River Saguenay

CANADA
QUEBEC

Quebec

St. Lawrence River

St. Lawrence Seaway

United States

Lake Champlain

Boston

ATLANTIC OCEAN

Montreal

Ottawa

Ottawa River

CANADA
ONTARIO

LAKE ONTARIO

Erie Canal

Hudson River

New York City

Pennsylvania

Lake Nipissing

GEORGIAN BAY

Toronto

Niagara Falls

Buffalo

LAKE ERIE

Sault Ste. Marie
Saint Mary's River

Soo Locks

LAKE HURON

Cleveland

OHIO

MICHIGAN

Lake St. Clair

Detroit

Detroit River

Toledo

Bay City

MICHIGAN

Marquette

LAKE SUPERIOR

MICHIGAN

LAKE MICHIGAN

Gary

INDIANA

Chicago

Lake Nipigon

CANADA
Thunder Bay

WISCONSIN

ILLINOIS

United States

MINNESOTA

Duluth

Superior

N

95

Ribs for the sides of the boat and braces to hold the deck, called knees, were formed from strong pieces of wood by using an ax or adze. Then a good square timber was hewn from a tree to be used as a keel for the sailboat.

When the lumber had dried, a sailboat was built by fastening the pieces together with wooden pegs that were driven into holes bored into the timbers. Then the spaces between the planks on the vessel's sides were carefully caulked to keep water from coming into the hold of the vessel. When the sailboat was finished it was allowed to slide into the water of the river. It was then floated downstream to one of the Great Lakes. Then the sails were raised. Leaning to one side, as the wind billowed out her sails, another sailboat had entered the rapidly growing carrying trade on the Great Lakes. These little sailboats, as well as the new steamboats, were soon carrying settlers, with their horses, oxen, and wagons across Lake Erie to Michigan. They also carried furs, salted fish, smoked meat, lumber and grain as they returned eastward across the lake.

Steamboats were beginning to be built and the first one to sail on the upper lakes, called the Walk-in-the-Water, was built near Buffalo, New York. The Walk-in-the-Water made her first trip across Lake Erie to Detroit in 1818. The Walk-in-the-Water was about one hundred thirty-five feet long, thirty-two feet wide, and sank into the the water about eight and a half feet. On a trip from Buffalo to Detroit between thirty and forty cords of wood were burned to make steam in the boiler. This wood was bought by the steamship company from settlers who were clearing land in northern Ohio and southern Michigan. The fare from Buffalo to Detroit was eighteen dollars. It took a day and a half to two days to make the trip one way. Stops were made at some of the new settlements along the south shore of Lake Erie. At some places the passengers and freight had to be carried from the boat to the shore on the backs of the sailors as the water was shallow and there were no docks. At some of the stops where there was a dock, more cord wood had to be loaded onto the boat to keep the fire burning to make steam to run the boat. After the Walk-in-the-Water other steamboats were built to carry the settlers and their products from the growing number of farms. These early steamboats played an important part in bringing settlers to southern Michigan.

Steamboats were more expensive to build and run than sailboats but they had advantages over the sailboats. They could leave at almost any time if the weather was good and not have to wait for a favorable wind. Because of this they could run on a more regular schedule. It was also easier for them to go up the Detroit and St. Clair rivers and into and out of ports.

But because of their low cost of construction and operation many sailboats were still built to carry lake shipping. The largest number of sailboats sailing the Great Lakes was in 1873. After that date the number of sailboats declined as the faster steamboats and railroads carried more of the growing east-west traffic. Many of the sailboats were demasted and used for several years as freight and lumber barges that were towed behind the new, faster steam freighters. The last freight-carrying sailboat on the Great Lakes, called "Our Son," sank on Lake Michigan in 1932.

Although the railroads, which ran trains even in the wintertime, began carrying more and more freight and passengers, lake shipping especially of bulk cargoes like grain, limestone, coal, and iron ore, has remained one of our major means of transportation in the Great Lakes area.

To Check Your Reading

1. What was the name of the first steamboat on Lake Erie?

2. What kind of wood was used for the ribs and sides of the early boats?

3. What wood was used for the masts? Can you tell why?

4. How were some of the early sailboats built? What kind of freight did they carry?

5. What was the peak year for commercial sailboats on the Great Lakes?

6. What was cord wood? For what was it used? Look in your dictionary to find out how large a cord of wood is.

7. What advantages do steam boats have over sailboats?

Things to Talk About and Do

1. Read **Ships of the Great Lakes,** by James Barry to find out more about them.

2. Why is it cheaper to ship goods by boat than any other way?

The Saint Mary's Falls Ship Canal

The Saint Mary's River flows from Lake Superior to Lake Huron which is about twenty-two feet below the Lake Superior level. About eighteen feet of this difference in water level lies in a small area where the run off water leaves Lake Superior. Here the water flows over a Cambrian sandstone ledge that forms a rapids in the river that the French explorers named the Sault.

All early travelers using the voyageur's highway to and from Lake Superior had to portage all freight and canoes for about one mile beside the rapids in the river. In 1796, the Northwest Fur Company built a small canal on the Canadian side of the river just large enough to allow the passage of the small boats and canoes then used in the western fur trade. This canal was destroyed by the Americans during the War of 1812. So again all freight had to be portaged overland on wagons, sleighs or on men's backs.

Soon after Michigan became a state the state legislature granted $25,000.00

for making surveys and plans for a canal beside the rapids. Because of the financial panic of 1837 and other difficulties, the plan for a canal was dropped. When the United States government was asked to aid in building a canal congress refused because its members saw no need for a canal so far to the north from the western settlements.

When iron ore and copper began to be mined in the Upper Peninsula a better means of transportation around the rapids had to be developed to carry these minerals to market. Congress then became interested in building a canal beside the Saint Mary's rapids. Seventy-five thousand acres of government land were sold to get money to pay for the building of the canal. Some of the land was mineral land in the western part of the Upper Peninsula but much of the land that was sold was some of Michigan's best pine forest land that lumbermen were then becoming interested in buying.

Work on the canal was started in 1853. Because the canal was far from the railroads and settlements at that time, all supplies had to be brought there by boat during the summertime when the lakes were open. It was hard to cut the rock with the tools of that time. The long cold winter weather also delayed work on the canal. Mr. Charles Harvey was in charge of building the canal and locks and in spite of the cold weather and hardships kept his men steadily at work. Much of the work in building the canal was done by immigrants who had come to Michigan to find work. Many of these immigrants were Irishmen. In April 1855, the canal was completed and boats could now

pass between Lake Superior and Lake Huron.

There were two locks in this first canal. Each one was three hundred feet long and had a depth of thirteen feet. One lock led into the other. Each lock lifted a boat about nine feet. From 1855 to 1881, the canal was run by the state of Michigan and tolls were collected on the tonnage passing through the locks. Since 1881, the canal has been operated by the United States government and no tolls are now charged. Although the locks in the canal were large enough for the small boats, they were soon found to be too small to permit the passage of the larger ore carriers that were being built to carry the growing commerce of the lakes. Since that time other and larger locks have been built.

The St. Mary's Falls Canal at Sault Ste. Marie, Michigan.

Today, there are four American, and one Canadian, locks at Sault Ste. Marie. The newest lock to replace the older Poe Lock was finished in 1968. It is now the largest of the "Soo" locks. It is twelve hundred feet long, one hundred feet wide and thirty-two feet deep. During the shipping season on the Great Lakes, large lake boats and foreign ships use these locks as they carry their cargoes of grain, iron ore, limestone, cement, coal and foreign imports. So large is the amount of traffic passing through the "Soo" locks that it is one of the world's busiest waterways.

A lock is really a water elevator that raises or lowers a boat from one water level to another. When a boat is to be raised from a lower water level to a higher one, gate B is opened and the boat moves to position C. Then gate B is closed. Water is then pumped into the space between gates A and B. As the water rises between gates A and B the boat rises to position D. When the water level between gates A and B is level with that of the higher lake, gate A is opened and the boat moves out upon the higher lake.

If a boat is to be lowered to a lower level, the space between A and B is filled with water. Gate A is then opened and the boat moves into position D. Gate A is then closed. The water between gates A and B is then allowed to run into the lower lake. As the water leaves, the boat is lowered to position C. When the water between gates A and B is the same level as that of the lower lake, or river, gate B is opened and the boat can move out of the lock.

The Saint Mary's Falls Ship Canal

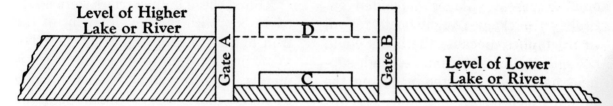

Can You Answer These Questions About the Saint Mary's Falls Ship Canal?

1. Why do locks sometimes have to be built to permit boats to go from one water level to another?

2. What is a lock? How does it work?

3. How was freight carried around the Saint Mary's Falls before 1855?

4. Who was in charge of building the locks at the "Soo"?

5. What shipping need made the building of the locks at the "Soo" necessary?

6. How was the cost of building the locks paid?

7. Who pays for the present cost of operating the locks at the "Soo"?

8. How many locks were there in the first canal?

9. How many locks are there at the "Soo" at the present time?

Problems and Reports

1. What books can you find in your library that tell about the "Soo" canal? One would be **The Pictorial History of the Great Lakes** by Hatcher and Walter.

2. Another reference about the Soo is the **Michigan History** magazine, January/February 1981 issue, page 9. (Vol. 65 - Number 1.)

3. What can you find out about the Welland Canal that permits boats to pass from Lake Ontario to Lake Erie?

4. Be able to locate Sault Ste. Marie, the Saint Mary's River, Lake Superior and Lake Huron on your map of Michigan.

The Bulk Freight Carriers

At first most of the freight that the boats carried was called package freight; such as, bundles of furs, barrels of fish or flour, sacks of grain, barrels of pork, or boxes of merchandise. Before the railroads were built to supply the port towns and mining communities, these villages depended entirely on package freight boats for all their supplies. Because the boats could not sail in the wintertime, enough supplies had to be brought in during the shipping season on the lakes to last through the coming winter.

As the years passed most of the package freight began to be carried by the railroads. Bulk cargoes became the freight that the boats carried. The first bulk cargo on the lakes was grain. Later bulk cargoes of iron ore, limestone, lumber, and coal also began to be carried. To carry the bulk cargoes new and better boats were designed and built especially for the iron ore carrying trade.

At first these bulk carriers were made of wood. With the development of the iron and steel industry after the Civil War, boats began to be made of these metals. By using steel, it was possible to make much larger boats than the earlier ones which had been made of wood.

One unusual type of these early bulk iron ore carriers was called a whaleback. It was shaped like a large cigar with the engine room and pilot house rising above the deck in the stern of the boat. When loaded it sank so low in the water that waves, during a storm, passed freely over the deck. Because whalebacks carried only a small amount of iron ore and were difficult to unload, their place in the carrying trade was taken by larger and better designed ore carriers.

The boats that were developed for iron ore carriers were from six to eight hundred feet long and about sixty or seventy feet wide. This was as large

An upbound freighter leaving the MacArthur Lock at the "Soo."

as they could be built and yet pass through the locks at the "Soo" at that time. In the stern, or back of the boat, was the engine room where the coal was kept to burn to make steam in the boilers, quarters for most of the men, and the propeller that pushed the boat through the water. Ahead of the stern was the hold of the carrier in which the cargo of iron ore, or coal, was carried. Above the hold, on the boat's deck, were large doors, called hatches, through which the iron ore was put into the hold of the carrier. Up in the bow, or front of the boat, was the pilot house, officers' quarters, and some storage space for supplies. In the pilot house was the large wheel that the pilot used to steer the boat. Here also were the compass and other instruments used for guiding the boat.

To load the iron ore into the ore carriers, large ore docks were built at Marquette and Escanaba. Ore cars, filled with iron ore from the mines, were pushed out onto the top of the ore dock. When the doors in the bottom of the cars were opened the ore dropped into huge bins in the ore dock. When an ore carrier was to be loaded it was run alongside one of these docks. Long chutes, attached to the sides of the ore dock, were then lowered through the open hatches of the boat and into the hold. The iron ore was then allowed to slide down the chute and into the hold of the ore carrier. To load an ore carrier in this way took only a few hours.

When one of the early ore carriers reached port, the hatches were opened so that the ore could be taken from the boat. At first men working in the hold of the boat shoveled the iron ore into large buckets that were then hoisted to the boat's deck by means of rope, pulleys, and teams of horses. Then the ore was wheeled, by men, from the boat to the dock. To unload a boat in this way was too slow. Later, machines called unloaders, that lifted as much as twenty tons of ore at a time were developed to unload the freighters. When the ore was raised from a boat it was some-

The James R. Barker is one of the larger new boats coming into service on the Great Lakes. It is one of the largest vessels ever built entirely on the Great Lakes. The James R. Barker is 1,000 feet long, 105 feet wide with a depth of 28 feet. It has a capacity of 59,000 tons of taconite pellets.   Courtesy, Pickands Mather & Co.

101

times piled alongside the dock for use in a local steel plant but most of the ore reaching the ports on the southern shore of Lake Erie was loaded into railroad cars and taken to the furnaces down along the Ohio River.

Since about 1900, these boats have been the carriers for bringing iron ore from the upper part of Michigan, Wisconsin, and Minnesota to the ports on the south shore of Lake Michigan and Lake Erie. About ninety percent of the iron ore comes from Minnesota. About one eighth of the ore goes to the southern end of Lake Michigan to ports in Indiana and Illinois. Ports on the southern shore of Lake Erie receive the other seven-eighths.

After 1960, when Canadian ore began to be shipped up the St. Lawrence Waterway to compete with ore from the Lake Superior area and new taconite plants were developed in other areas of the United States, many of the older, smaller and slower iron ore carriers were taken out of service. A few of them have been remodeled into other types of carriers. Over eighty of them, Canadian and American, have been sold for scrap iron to companies in Europe. They were taken down the Saint Lawrence Waterway and towed across the Atlantic Ocean by sea going tugs. Some of them sank in the Atlantic while being towed.

There are fewer ships working on the Great Lakes today because of the recent decline in the steel industry. Less than half of the approximately one hundred American-owned ships on the Lakes are in operation.

Because of the enlarged Poe Lock, opened in 1968 at the "Soo," new and larger ore carriers are now being built that are 1,000 feet long, 105 feet wide, with a draft of 26 feet nine inches. Because much of the ore now being carried on the Great Lakes is taconite pellets some of the new ore boats now being built are self-unloaders. These new boats will carry 55,000 tons of iron ore. Even larger ones, carrying about 100,000 tons are now in service on the oceans carrying iron ore and petroleum.

The self-unloaders on the Great Lakes are usually not as large. Their size allows them to go into many of the smaller ports to deliver their cargoes. They can carry limestone, gravel and gypsum in addition to ore and coal.

On the deck of each of these self-unloaders is a large boom that can be swung out over the side of the boat at

A self-unloader. These boats carry coal, limestone and salt.

a forty-five degree angle. One or two endless belts, in the hold, carry the salt, coal, or limestone forward. Then the cargo is raised on an elevator made up of buckets on another belt. The buckets then dump the cargo onto another endless belt that carries the cargo onto the boom that is over the boat's side. The cargo moves out on the boom from where it falls to the ground.

To Check Your Reading

1. What were package freighters?
2. What kind of items made up package freight?
3. What is meant by bulk cargo?
4. What did whalebacks look like?
5. What material replaced wood for building boats? Why?
6. Describe the looks of an iron ore carrier.
7. What does the pilot of a boat do?
8. What has happened to many of the older ore carriers?
9. How large are the new ore carriers that are now being built?
10. What change in the "Soo" locks has made it possible to use larger lake boats?
11. What is a self-unloader? What type of cargo do they carry?

Things to Do and Talk About

1. During the shipping season some of Michigan's newspapers list the vessel passages at Detroit and Sault Ste. Marie. If your paper has such a list bring it to class. Does it report the arrival or departure of any foreign ships?
2. Watch your paper during the shipping season for items on Great Lakes shipping. Some papers run a weekly column telling about boats on the lakes.
3. What is meant by the draft of a boat?

Dangers of the Lakes

A November storm was brewing on Lake Superior. The freighter, Edmund Fitzgerald, was hauling taconite ore pellets from Superior, Wisconsin, to Detroit. Close behind her was the Arthur Anderson, another ore freighter. The Anderson radioed the Fitzgerald at 7:10 p.m. to tell them that another ship was about nine miles ahead. The radar was not working on the Fitzgerald, so the Anderson was trying to help. The wind was blowing at nearly ninety miles an hour, and the waves were now reaching eighteen feet. The Edmund Fitzgerald was taking on water, and the pumps were working hard to remove it.

The mate on the Anderson reported a few minutes later that he could see the lights of the boat coming from the other direction, but he could not see the Fitzgerald! A check on the radar showed that the freighter had disappeared!

The Anderson turned around to look for the Fitzgerald, and soon the other passing freighters began to help in spite of the storm. Within a few hours, Coast Guard helicoptors and planes were looking too. However, it was all too late for the twenty-nine crewmen of the once great freighter. All were now in a watery grave 530 feet beneath the surface of the lake, and the freighter was twisted into two pieces.

Many sailors have ideas as to what caused such a large ship to sink so quickly, but no one knows for sure.

The Great Lakes have always been dangerous to ships and sailors.

In another November storm in 1913, seventeen ships sank in one day! In most cases there were no survivors.

Probably the fact that shocks people the most about the sinking of the Edmund Fitzgerald is that it took place in 1975, when modern radar, radio, lifeboats, search planes and helicoptors were all available. All of the modern equipment was not enough to make the lakes safe.

Remember, as you stand on the shore of any of the Great Lakes, that the lake you see before you can be like a peacefully sleeping giant who may awaken and unleash terrible power in the form of winds and waves. No matter how powerful man thinks he is, the Great Lakes will always be a mighty force with which to reckon.

To Check Your Reading

1. What kind of ship was the Edmund Fitzgerald?

2. What cargo was it carrying when it sank?

3. Were there any survivors?

4. Is it true that only one or two ships have sunk on the Great Lakes?

Things to Do and Talk About

1. The Fitzgerald sank seventeen miles northwest of Whitefish Point in Lake Superior. Find this point on a map.

2. Research from books or old newspapers some of the probable causes of the sinking. These books may help you — **The Wreck of the Edmund Fitzgerald,** by Frederick Stonehouse; and **Great Lakes Shipwrecks,** by William Ratigan.

3. Find out information about other Great Lakes shipwrecks. These books by Captain Dana Bowen may help you. **Shipwrecks of the Lakes, Lore of the Lakes, Memories of the Lakes.**

Two of the last passenger boats docked at Detroit. Soon after this picture was taken they were towed into Lake St. Clair and burned. Photo, 1956.

For many years large boats known as railroad car ferries carried railroad cars across Lake Michigan between Michigan and Wisconsin; but during the last few years this ferry service has greatly declined. Railroad car ferry service across the Straits of Mackinac between Mackinaw City and St. Ignace stopped in 1984. Railroad car ferries for many years carried railroad cars across the Detroit River between Detroit and Windsor, Ontario. Today some railroad cars because of their height are still taken across the river on barges towed by tugs. Most railroad cars use the railroad tunnel under the Detroit River.

Another type of boat to be found on the Great Lakes is the tanker. These boats carry petroleum products to ports on the upper Great Lakes to places where the pipe lines do not run. In this way petroleum products like gasoline and heating oil are carried to the upper part of the state.

Other Great Lakes Boats

From 1818 to 1955 passenger steamers carried thousands of people and much package freight during the summer shipping season. These passenger boats ran on a regular time schedule. The heaviest traffic was between Detroit, Cleveland and Buffalo. Other boats made regular runs to Alpena, Mackinac Island, Duluth, Charlevoix, Chicago and other lake ports. The boats were provided with rooms in which the passengers slept during the night. Large cabins, with windows through which the passengers could view the lake and passing boats, were ornate with carved wood and colored glass. Dining rooms and ball rooms, for dancing, were also provided for the passengers.

Other boats called vacation cruise boats also carried passengers. These boats took cruises that lasted from a day or two to ten days or more. The boats stopped at several places around the lakes. Often they stayed at each place long enough for the passengers to spend a few hours sight seeing. The last of these vacation cruise boats was the South American that, after fifty-three years of service, stopped running in October 1967.

Up to about 1930, several smaller boats ran from Detroit each day to picnic areas; such as, "Bob-lo," Sugar Island, Put-in-Bay, or Tashmoo Park on Harsens Island. The only one of these boats that is still running is the one that goes to "Bob-lo" from Detroit. Bob-lo is a Canadian island in the lower Detroit River.

To break the ice in the lakes in the spring and fall, boats called ice breakers are used. They are operated by the United States Coast Guard. The largest ice breaker on the Great Lakes today is

The ice breaker Mackinaw. Ice breakers are used to open the shipping lanes in the spring. Photo, 1957.

the Mackinaw which is stationed at Cheboygan. Each spring the Mackinaw breaks the ice in the Saint Mary's River and Whitefish Bay on Lake Superior so that freighters can begin another shipping season. Other smaller ice breakers are also stationed at other ports around the Great Lakes.

Today, shipping on the Great Lakes is controlled by the federal government. The government aids shipping in many ways besides operating the Saint Mary's Falls Ship Canal. The Army Corps of Engineers dredges channels leading into many ports so that boats can enter. Each spring the Coast Guard places buoys in dangerous places to mark the shipping lanes. In the fall these buoys

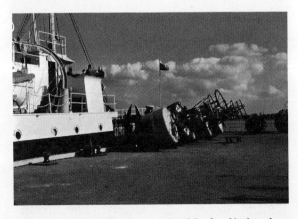

Each spring buoys like this are placed in the shipping channels to guide the sailors on the Great Lakes.

are removed and repaired for the next shipping season.

For over one hundred years, lighthouses along the shores of the Great Lakes were used by sailors to guide their boats through narrow channels or to keep them away from dangerous shores or reefs. Several lighthouses were manned by men all during the shipping season. Now with radar to warn the crew of a boat there is no longer a need for many of these lighthouses. Several have been abandoned; while others now have automatic lights and fog horns to warn sailors of danger.

For several years small foreign ships, that did not sink more than fourteen feet in the water, have been coming up the canal system along the St. Lawrence River in Canada to ports on the Great Lakes. But since the opening of the new and deeper St. Lawrence Waterway in 1959, larger foreign ships, not sinking in the water more than twenty-seven feet, have been coming up the St. Lawrence Waterway to ports on the Great Lakes. Each year these ships bring goods from foreign lands and carry away American products. One of the main exports carried to foreign lands by these ships is wheat from western Canada and the United States. Logs, chemicals, and machinery parts are also exported from Canada and the United States. Special ships are now being built in Europe for this new St. Lawrence Waterway shipping. These ships are strengthened as ice breakers for early and late season service on the waterway. Besides carrying bulk cargo these ships carry cargoes such as beans from Saginaw in large containers to protect the shipment from spillage.

Reading Checks

1. Where was most of the passenger traffic carried on the lakes?
2. What were vacation cruise boats?
3. What is an ice breaker?
4. What is the name of the largest of the ice breakers on the lakes? Where is she stationed?
5. In what ways does the United States government aid shipping on the Great Lakes?
6. How has the St. Lawrence Waterway aided foreign shipping on the Great Lakes?

Some Things to Think About

1. What do you think caused the passenger boats to stop running?
2. Listen to the cassette tape **The Great Steamboat Race** on the Voices from Michigan's Past Series (Aural Press).
3. Why are boats safer today than they were fifty years ago?

Top: The way to travel in 1908. These people are boarding steamers in Port Huron. When these boats ran along the same routes there was often rivalry and races. (Library of Congress)

Bottom: Here we have a young sailor at the Detroit Boat Club near the turn of the Century. (Library of Congress)

Recent Changes In Great Lakes Shipping

The Poe Lock in the Saint Mary's Falls Ship Canal at Sault Ste. Marie, was enlarged and opened in 1968. Now, new and larger boats are being built for service on the Great Lakes. Some of these new carriers are 1,000 feet long, 105 feet wide and sink into the water about thirty feet when loaded. These new boats can carry as much as 55,000 tons of iron ore, which is more than twice the cargo carried by the older boats for so many years. Since they carry taconite pellets, they are self-unloaders and do not have to use the Hulett unloaders to unload their cargo. On the older carriers the pilot house was in the bow of the boat but on these newer ore boats the pilot house is in the stern along with the sailors' quarters and the machinery. Unlike the older boats that were steam driven, these new carriers are motor driven. Because of their depth when fully loaded, they can not go down the Detroit River at present because of the depth of the Livingstone Channel. When carrying a full load they bring iron ore from Lake Superior to the southern end of Lake Michigan. Only a few ports on the Great Lakes are deep enough to allow these new carriers to enter and discharge their cargo.

Coal from Ohio has been one of the major bulk cargoes carried on the Great Lakes for many years. Ore carriers returning up to Lake Superior often carried coal to ports on Lake Superior. Small self-unloaders have carried coal to ports along the Great Lakes.

Because of the energy crisis the United States is turning to the use of coal as a future source of power. In Wyoming, and Montana, states in the upper part of the Western United States, also in Canada, there are vast quantities of low sulphur coal that can be secured by strip mining. Today, trans-shipment facilities have been built at Thunder Bay, Ontario, and at Superior, Wisconsin. The one at Superior, Wisconsin, is called the Superior Midwest Energy Terminal. Long trains with 110-car units are bringing this coal to the terminal at Superior. During the winter the coal is stock-piled for later shipment during the lake shipping season. New large boats, called colliers, have been built to carry this coal from Superior, Wisconsin to the Detroit Edison Company power plant at St. Clair. The colliers also bring coal from Ohio to Detroit.

How Well Did You Read?
1. Where is the Poe Lock located? When was the enlarged Poe Lock opened for shipping?
2. Name three ways in which the newer boats are different from the older boats.
3. Why has coal been shipped up the lakes? How was it carried?
4. Why will much coal now be shipped down the lakes?

Things to Do and Talk About
1. What are the advantages and disadvantages of having really large freighters on the Lakes?
2. Be able to locate the following on a map of the United States: Superior, Wisconsin; Sault Ste. Marie, Michigan; and the states of Montana and Wyoming.

Chapter 11

Changes in Land Transportation

The First Roads in Michigan

When France and England controlled the Great Lakes area there were no roads in Michigan as we have today. Only a few muddy roads ran in or close to the few settlements. Through the forests and swamps there were some animal paths which the Indians sometimes followed.

When settlers began coming to Michigan it was along these Indian trails that they often made their first roads. Later they were straightened and widened, by clearing away the trees, so that horses or oxen could pull two-wheel carts or wagons along them. Between Detroit and the new settlements in Ohio lay a large swamp, known as the "Black Swamp," around the western end of Lake Erie. In 1812, General Hull's army cut a road through this swamp as the army came toward Detroit. Later another road was cut from this one toward the east along the southern shore of Lake Erie that led on to present day Pittsburgh. Although a poor one, this road from present day Toledo to Detroit was the first real road in Michigan. Today it is U.S. 25. In 1816, soldiers began improving this road which was then called the River Road. In 1823, a stage coach line began running stage coaches along this road. It was finished in 1829.

Many of the main streets in Detroit were once Indian trails that led out into different parts of the state. Between 1818 and 1835, as settlers began coming to Michigan, the federal government cut new roads along these Indian trails so that settlers could move into the state. These main roads ran out from Detroit like the spokes on half a wheel. One called the Chicago Road ran through Ypsilanti, Saline, Clinton, Coldwater, Sturgis, Niles, and then to New Buffalo. It is now U.S. 12. Another ran from Detroit to the Grand River, at Lansing, and was called the Grand River Road. It ran through Novi, Brighton, Howell and Williamston. Another ran north to Saginaw and passed through Pontiac and Flint. Still another was made from Detroit to Fort Gratiot at what is now Port Huron. From these main roads still poorer ones led off into the forest often along section lines that were being laid out by men surveying the state.

Although these roads aided the settlement of southern Michigan they were really built as military roads for the movement of soldiers and military supplies. Until the interstate highways were built these roads were some of Michigan's main highways.

Old 27 and the railroad from Saginaw to Mackinaw City followed an old Indian trail. This is true also of the road and railroad from Grand Rapids to Mackinaw City. In the Upper Peninsula U.S. 2 from Sault Ste. Marie to Escanaba, and M35, from Escanaba to Menominee, follow the old Sault and Green Bay trail.

These early roads were not well made. Often they were little more than lanes cut through the forest. Little grading and drainage was done. When it rained the roads became very muddy, especially near Detroit where the heavy clay was very sticky. Water stood in the pools made by the horses' hoofs and in the long narrow troughs made by the wagon wheels. Through the mud the horses and oxen struggled as they dragged the wagons and stage coaches after them.

During the dry weather the clay hardened and then the roads became rough and the wagons bumped along. To haul heavy loads any distance was hard if not impossible.

So poor were these roads that pioneers often took three days to go from Detroit to Ypsilanti, a distance of only twenty-eight miles. Over these roads the early settlers made their way into the wilderness.

Stage coach lines began running on roads leading out from Detroit. Usually the coaches were drawn by four or six horses. At night these stage coaches stopped at little inns along the way.

In 1827, a law passed by the Michigan Territory made the townships responsible for all roads except for the main ones built by the federal government. Thus, road building was a local affair.

In 1837, when Michigan became a state, the new state had little money to spend and road building was still the duty of the townships. Canals and railroads were the means of transportation that people were thinking about. The Erie Canal was proving to be a success. Canals, running across the state, and railroads were planned and started by the state at state expense.

Stagecoaches managed to make regular runs over the dust, mud and bumpy planks of early roads. Passengers certainly didn't travel in comfort!

While the state was interested in canals and railroads, private companies tried to build better roads. In 1844, a charter was granted for the building of one of the first plank roads in Michigan. It was to run from Detroit to Port Huron. In 1848, the state passed the Plank Road Act. Plank roads were to be eight feet wide and three inches thick. These roads were made possible because of the better and easier way of sawing lumber and because of the vast amount of hardwood that was near at hand. A plank road was built between Detroit and Pontiac. Another ran from Detroit to Howell. One also ran between Flint and Saginaw. Any one who used the plank roads had to pay for their use. A two horse wagon paid two cents a mile. A one horse wagon paid one cent a mile. To take twenty cattle one mile cost two cents. Plank roads were not a success. The planks rotted rapidly and wore away with use as hoofs and wheels passed over them. When new planks were put in to replace the old ones, they were higher than the worn ones and thus made the road bumpy.

To Check Your Reading

1. What was land transportation like in this area during the French and English periods?

2. What was the Black Swamp? Where was it located? Who made a road across this swamp?

3. Many of the early roads were not built for the settlers. Why were they built?

4. Where did the following roads run? 1. Fort Gratiot Road? 2. The Saginaw Road? 3. The Grand River Road? 4. The Chicago Road? Show these roads on your outline map of Michigan.

5. How well were these early roads made?

6. Long ago how much time did it take to go from Detroit to Ypsilanti?

7. What was a plank road? Why were they built? Where were some of these early plank roads built? How successful were they?
   (See **Vanishing Landscape,** by Eric Sloane for more information.)

Things to Do and Talk About

1. What can you find out about Michigan's Indian trails? early roads? early inns? traveling in early Michigan? An excellent reference is **The Chronicle,** Spring-1981, pages 27-33. (Volume 17, No. 1)

2. Read "Michigan's Historic Highways" in **Michigan Living,** January, 1987.

Rail Transportation

Railroads were built in Michigan even before Michigan became a state. As early as 1830, a group of men were granted permission to build a railroad from Detroit to Pontiac. But the first one to be built was the Erie and Kalamazoo which was built from Toledo, Ohio, to Adrian. Service began in the fall of 1836.

In April 1836, work was started on a railroad to run from Detroit to Pontiac. In that same year work was started on another to run from Detroit west across the state to St. Joseph. It was to be called the Detroit and St. Joseph Railroad.

When Michigan became a state in 1837, the state legislature voted fifteen million dollars for building three railroads that were to be owned by the state. The Michigan Northern was to run across the state from Port Huron to Grand Haven, on Lake Michigan. The Michigan Central was to run across the state from Detroit to St. Joseph. This line was already being built under the name of the Detroit and St. Joseph Railroad. It was bought by the state and renamed the Michigan Central. In 1838, trains were running as far as Ypsilanti. In 1839, it reached Ann Arbor, in 1844 Albion, in 1845 Battle Creek, and in 1846 Kalamazoo. The Michigan Southern was to run from Monroe to New Buffalo, on Lake Michigan.

Michigan's railroad building program was part of the wild speculation that brought on the Panic of 1837. For a time it looked as if the state itself would be unable to pay its debts. By 1846, Michigan was ready to sell her interest in the railroads. Buyers were found and the railroads passed into private ownership.

The early railroads were far different from the ones that may pass near your home today. The tracks upon which the trains ran were made of wooden rails. Over the tops of the wooden rails were placed long iron strips upon which the wheels of the engine and cars ran. The engines were small and usually had only one pair of driving wheels. Behind the engine came a car that looked like a wagon. On this car wood was piled. During the run the fireman carried the wood forward to the engine and threw it into the fire to keep up the steam in the boiler. These engines had large smokestacks. With each puff of the little engine huge sparks from the fire went flying up the stack. Fires were often started by these flying sparks. To stop this a screen was placed over the top of each engine stack to keep the burning wood from flying out.

Behind the engine came the passenger coaches. They were really stage coaches put upon the rails. The freight cars had only four wheels each. The axles on the engine and the coaches were the same width as were the wagon axles of that day. That distance became known as "standard gauge" (four feet eight and one-half inches). Today railroad rails are laid the same distance from each other.

In order for the railroads to get settlers to come by the way of Detroit, on their way west, the Michigan Central Railroad ran large passenger boats on Lake Erie for a few years. Passengers would be carried from Buffalo, New York, on one of these boats. Then they would go across the state on one of the passenger trains. From there they would again go by boat to Chicago.

After 1860, more railroads were built in the state, especially in the upper part of the Lower Peninsula and in the Upper Peninsula. Both the national government and the state government helped in the building of these lines by giving the railroad companies grants of land on each side of the track. Sometimes the railroad companies were granted land in every section of land that the railroad passed through. Some smaller lines joined with larger ones to make the railroad companies that we know today.

Before better roads began to be built the railroad lines provided the best means of transportation. Settlers used them to get goods from the cities and also to ship their farm produce to market. Logging companies used them to carry their saw logs to the mills. Many of the railroads, built to aid in lumbering, did much to aid in the settlement of the upper part of the Lower Peninsula and the Upper Peninsula. Railroads provided the cheapest and fastest means of transportation that had been known.

From 1850 to 1935, railroads were the main overland freight carriers. Many changes were made during this time by the railroad companies. T rails, made of the new Bessemer steel, replaced the earlier strap rails. Large steam engines, capable of pulling one hundred cars, replaced the earlier engines. Passenger cars were made larger and more comfortable. Special cars to carry coal, logs, cattle, gasoline, refrigerated meats, fruits, baggage and general freight were built. Passenger trains, running on a regular schedule, carried people from station to station.

In 1910, there were about nine thousand miles of railroad tracks in Michigan. As the years passed, however, less timber was cut, better roads were built, people began using the new automobiles, and trucks began to carry freight. Many railroads found that there was less traffic and that they were losing money. So, many of the branch lines going to declining lumber towns or mining communities, were abandoned and the rails taken up. By 1947, there were only about seven thousand miles of railroad tracks left in the state. Since that time nearly all of the passenger trains have been taken out of service. Many towns now have an abandoned passenger and freight depot at which people no longer wait for passenger trains to come. On some of the railroads, that were once busy lines, now only an occasional freight train is run.

The use of railroads has now started to increase somewhat. Improved passenger trains run by Amtrak link some Michigan cities. Several railroads are improving their tracks and equipment with the help of state aid. Although most of the railroads are not as busy as they were fifty years ago some still play a major part in Michigan's commerce especially in the field of bulk freight; such as, coal, grain and in transporting automobiles.

One of the major changes in railroads during the last few years is the development of unit trains. In unit trains all the cars are alike and are coupled together by couplings that turn so that one car at a time can be dumped as it passes a certain place. This reduces the cost of unloading. These trains are used to haul coal and iron ore. Usually they are about one hundred cars in length. Another major change has been the replacing of the earlier steam engines by diesel engines. Special cars carry loaded truck trailers on top of long flatcars. This is called "piggy back."

In the 1890's special lines called interurbans became popular. These used self-powered cars so that a train could be made of only one car. The interurbans were used on shorter trips, usually less than one hundred miles. Most major cities had interurban service. In 1918 there were 1,747 miles of interurban lines in the state.

After 1900 street car lines were built in several cities. The street car and the interurban gave much needed service to the people. The interurbans ran every hour or two during the day and late into the night. This regular service from city to city made it easier for people to go from one city to another. People living near the cities would ride to work on them in the morning and then back home again at night. But the coming of better roads and automobiles gave people still better transportation and the interurbans and street cars stopped running.

How Well Did You Read?

1. What was the name of the first railroad to be built in Michigan? Where did it run?

2. Why did the state give up its plans for building railroads?

3. What were these early railroads like? Describe an early train.

4. What is "standard gauge"? Is it still being used?

5. How did the government aid in building the early railroads?

6. How did the railroads aid in the settlement of the state? How did they help its early development?

7. What are unit trains? Why are they used?

8. Why did railroad traffic decline?

9. What were interurban lines?

10. What new means of transportation affected the railroads and interurban lines?

Things to Do and Talk About

1. Look in the **Atlas of Michigan** and see what railroads run near your town (p. 214). Try to estimate the amount of freight carried on them by using the map.

2. Watch a freight train. How many railroad lines, whose names appear on the sides of the cars, can you name?

3. What kind of freight is hauled on the railroad near your home? Does it run as many freight and passenger trains as it did thirty years ago? Did this line carry different freight fifty years ago?

4. What improvements have been made in railroads and railroad transportation since the first railroads were built?

5. If you have taken a trip on a train tell the class about it.

6. What bus line runs near your home? Where do the buses go?

7. Why are railroads called railroads?

8. Can you find out how a steam engine works? If you can, tell the class what you have learned.

Better Roads Are Built

Until about 1890, most of the roads in Michigan were township roads. At that time there were only about two hundred miles of gravel and macadam roads in all of Michigan. All the remaining roads were still sand, or clay, and poorly drained. Many of them in the northern part of the state were still ungraded trails through the cut-over lands.

These township roads were supposed to be cared for by the people living along the road. Each taxpayer could pay his tax by working so many days each year on the road or paying cash for his share of the tax. People who were not tax payers were to give one day's work or pay a man's wages for one day's work. But township roads were usually in poor condition.

In hopes of making better roads the state legislature passed the County Road Act of 1893. This act made it possible for a county to have a county road system. Better road making machinery could now be bought for making and maintaining roads.

Because of the system of land survey, many of Michigan's roads in the southern part of the state were laid out along section lines parallel to each other and one mile apart. Their direction was only

changed when lakes or swamps made it necessary to run the roads around them. Many of these roads are gravel roads today.

By 1900, most people had bicycles that they rode to work and on pleasure trips into the country. A few people already owned automobiles. Those who owned bicycles and automobiles wanted to ride in the country and were soon asking that better roads be built. But, better roads would cost much money and that meant that people living in the cities would have to help pay the cost of building better roads. Bicycle clubs and the new automobile clubs began to work for better roads for Michigan.

In 1905, the Michigan State Highway Department was started. Those who owned automobiles were required to register them. A state wide system of highways began to be planned. By 1913, some sixty thousand automobiles were registered. In order to help pay the cost of building better roads, automobiles were to be taxed on their horse power and their weight. A three thousand mile main trunk line system was set up. In 1916 the federal government passed a Road Aid Act to help states build roads. As late as 1918 even main

Only fifty years after travelers were frustrated with terrible road conditions like these, Michigan had some of the best highways in the nation. (Henry Ford Museum)

highways were still gravel roads.

In 1925 a tax was placed on gasoline to get more money to keep in repair and to build state trunk lines. Since 1934 this tax has been the main support of the state trunk line system.

Today a system of state trunk lines spreads across the state. Each highway is designed, as well as it can be with limited funds, to carry the flow of traffic. Some main trunk lines are only two lanes wide. Some are four lanes and still others are four lane divided highways. These latter highways carry traffic the fastest and safest. Most of the main trunk lines lie south of Bay City and Grand Rapids. During the past few years the federal government has aided the states in their highway programs by paying much of the cost of building interstate highways. These highways are marked "I" and a number.

How Carefully Did You Read?

1. What were township roads? How were they built and cared for?

2. What was the County Road Act of 1893?

3. Why do many rural roads in the southern part of the state run parallel to each other?

4. What two means of transportation brought about the need for better roads?

5. When was the State Highway and Transportation Department started?

6. Why is there a tax on automobiles and gasoline?

7. Does an interstate highway run near your home? Name it.

8. Most of the main highways are south of what cities? Can you tell why?
    (Hint: Look in the **Atlas of Michigan** to see where most of the state's people live.)

Problems

1. What can you find out about the Michigan State Highway Department?

2. Are there any new roads being built near your home? Why?

3. How has the building of better roads helped the auto industry?

4. What is the county road commission? Who are the commissioners in your county? What do they do?

5. Sometimes people oppose the building of new highways in their area. What reasons might they have?

Map Work

Draw a map of your county and show on it the main roads, cities, and villages. Use a state highway map as a guide.

Modern Highways Serve Modern Needs

Rapid and easy transportation is part of our modern way of life. Today we have come to depend more and more upon our state system of roads. Each day thousands of gallons of fresh milk are carried by special trucks to cities and creameries. Rural mail carriers use thousands of miles of roads to deliver mail to people scattered all over the state in out of the way places. Today there are fewer Rural Free Delivery routes than there were in 1920 but the length has more than doubled. R.F.D. carriers in Michigan alone cover some fifty-five thousand miles each day.

One of the main reasons for the decline of the railroads during the past thirty years has been the rapid advance in highway building. Today much freight is hauled by trucks. Millions of dollars are invested in the trucking industry. Modern manufacturers use trucks for shipping their goods to market and for bringing raw materials to their plants. Cement, drugs, salt, paper products, chemicals, groceries, automobiles, and furniture, to mention a few items, are hauled to market in trucks. Before this, trains were used. Goods were left at the depot to be picked up. This extra stop made more work. Trucks can go almost anywhere, even to the customer's door. Perishable products get to market faster.

The farmer, as well as the manufacturer, has found that better all year hard surfaced roads have become a part of his way of life. In this way a farmer can sell his stock quickly and take advantage of market prices.

Michigan's system of roads makes possible her vast tourist industry. Each year during the summer months Michigan's highways are lined with cars filled with happy people taking their vacations. Michigan has four national forests covering some two million acres, several state forests covering some three and one-half million acres, about seventy-five state parks, thirty-six thousand miles of rivers, over eleven thousand lakes, and over three thousand miles of shoreline. Over two million acres of state forests are open to the public for hunting and fishing.

For several years the State Highway Department operated ferry boats across the Straits of Mackinac to carry automobiles and trucks between the two peninsulas. In November, 1957, this ferry service came to an end with the opening of the Mackinac Bridge that crosses the Straits from the Lower Peninsula, at Mackinaw City, to St. Ignace in the Upper Peninsula. This new bridge, called "Big Mac," is one of the largest bridges in the world. Over it one can quickly pass from one peninsula to the other. Each year thousands of people visit this area to see the bridge and the historic places that are nearby.

Modern highways also make it possible for Michigan to market many of her natural resources. Oil is refined and carried over highways to market. Cement is carried by huge trucks. Although the days of large scale lumbering have passed, timber is still produced in Michigan. Modern trucking methods for timber make small cuttings worth while.

Better fire protection is possible because better equipment can be hurried to a fire. All weather roads have brought better police protection and education as well. Since it has become easier to move around the state a system of State Police has been organized. In 1919 there were only twenty school buses in the state. Now hundreds of school buses pass over Michigan's highways twice each day carrying Michigan's students to better schools. Only a few one room grade schools are now left in the state.

Straits of Mackinac auto ferry "Vacationland." This was the largest and newest of the ferry fleet that stopped running in 1957.

To Check Your Reading

1. Why are good highways so important to our way of life?

2. What is Rural Free Delivery?

3. How have good roads aided industrial development? the farmers?

4. How do highways help to make Michigan a vacation land?
5. When did auto ferry service across the Straits of Mackinac stop? Why?
6. Between what two cities does the Mackinac Bridge run?
7. How have buses changed Michigan's schools?

Things to Do and Talk About

1. What modern highways run near your home?
2. How have the roads near your home changed in the past few years?
3. How do the roads near your home help the people of your community?
4. Do you know the Michigan traffic laws? How do you get a driver's license?
5. Why must our highways be made safer? How can we do this?

Finding Your Way By Car

The first time you decide to drive a car to another city is always an experience. It can be a good experience if you are familiar with the route, can read a map and can arrive without getting lost on the way. It may not be such a good experience if you suddenly find you are on a strange road and don't know what to do next, especially if it is a Detroit freeway during rush hour!

Michigan is crossed by several main highways. These provide the fastest way to get from one big city to another by car. There are three kinds of major highways: U.S. routes, state routes and interstates. The interstates are probably the best. They are divided highways with two or more lanes in each direction. State roads are developed and paid for by the state. The other two kinds of highways are supported by the federal government. On a map you can tell the three kinds of roads by the letter before the number. For example: **US**-12 is a United States route: **M**-28 is a state route (M for Michigan), and **I**-94 is an interstate route going between two or more states. It will be quite help-

ful if you know the numbers of these main highways, the direction they go, and the cities they connect.

I-94 is an interstate going across the southern part of the Lower Peninsula. It reaches from Detroit to Benton Harbor, and then goes on to Chicago. Along the way are Ann Arbor, Jackson, Battle Creek and Kalamazoo. I-96 is a little north of I-94. It connects Detroit, Lansing, Grand Rapids and Muskegon. An interstate running north from Detroit is I-75. It goes first to Flint, then Saginaw, Bay City, Grayling, Gaylord, the Mackinac Bridge, and then to Sault Ste. Marie.

US-127 and US-27 divide the Lower Peninsula of Michigan right down the middle and go through Jackson, Lansing, Mount Pleasant, and finally merge with I-75 near Grayling.

M-28 travels across the Upper Peninsula from near Sault Ste. Marie to Marquette and then to Ironwood. US-2 is a road that goes east-west across the Upper Peninsula. It is farther south than M-28.

There are many more roads and high-

Michigan's Major Highways

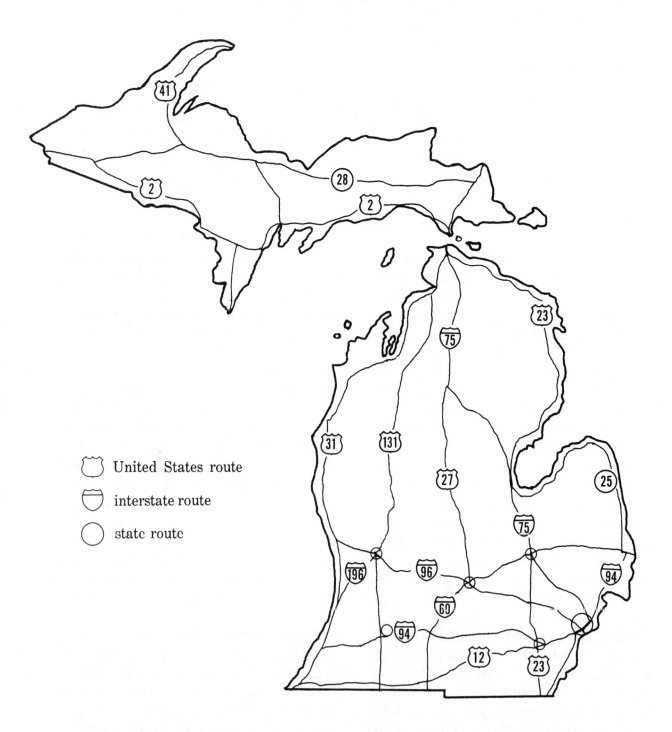

United States route

interstate route

state route

120

ways in our state. Look on a map and study them along with the ones already mentioned.

Something to remember while driving is to obey the speed limit. People often go faster and feel safe, but facts show that fewer people are killed or injured at the lower speeds. Once an accident happens, it is too late for a second chance!

To Check Your Reading

1. Which highways would you take to go from Lansing to Ann Arbor?
2. Which highway would you take to go from Detroit to the Mackinac Bridge?
3. Is it true that interstate routes are usually narrow roads often covered with gravel?

Thing to Do and Talk About

1. Going at the speed limit, find out how long it would take from where you live to drive to the following cities: Detroit, Lansing, Marquette and Sault Ste. Marie. What highways would you use to get to each of these cities from where you live?
2. Study Paul McCreary's book, **Michigan Map Skills and Information,** to learn more about how to read our state highway map.

Modern Air Travel

The most recent major change in transportation has been the rapid development of air travel. Michigan has played a part in this field but most of the airplanes have been made in other states. During World War I, when airplanes were just beginning to be used, wooden parts for airplane bodies were made at the furniture factories in Michigan. Airplane engines and mechanical parts were made at the automobile factories. For a few years after World War I the Ford Motor Company made an airplane called the Ford Tri-motor.

During World War II a large plant was built at Willow Run, near Ypsilanti, to make bombers. After World War II the automobile companies returned to making automobiles and let others build airplanes.

Commercial airlines, cargo lines and private planes fly a web that connects many Michigan cities. Planes reach out for Chicago, Cleveland and other cities in nearby states too. Detroit's Metropolitan Airport, known as Metro, is the largest in the state. If you have visited it, you know just how big it is — huge! It is not really in Detroit, but about twenty-one miles southwest of the city. Detroit and its suburbs have other smaller airports, but those are mostly used by private planes. The latest commercial jets are simply too big for them. If you sit in the observation area of the Metro Terminal, you can sometimes see a plane take off each minute. The planes may be going to Grand Rapids, Marquette, San Francisco, even London or Paris — nonstop! For many foreign travelers, Detroit's Metro Airport may be the first thing they see in the United States.

Much air freight is handled at Metro Airport besides the thousands of passengers going through there. Cargo, about 350 million pounds each year, is becoming a larger part of the air business in Michigan.

Grand Rapids has Michigan's second largest airport. Saginaw, Lansing, Flint, Muskegon and Kalamazoo have some of the other larger airports in the state.

Many cities and towns have small airports that are used mostly by private planes. About one-third of the flights from these are by people on business trips, and the remainder are for pleasure. More than ninety per cent of our population lives within a thirty minute drive of one airport or another.

To Check Your Reading

1. What was the Ford Tri-motor?
2. How did the auto industries help win World War I and World War II?
3. What is the name of Michigan's largest airport? Exactly where is it?
4. Where is our second largest airport located?
5. Is it true that each year more air business is the flying of cargo?

Things to Do and Talk About

1. Find out some of the foreign cities to which a person can fly directly from Detroit. (Check an airlines bulletin or ask at a travel agency.)
2. Find out the kind of flights that take off from the airport nearest you. Are they all private, some commercial, etc? What is the largest plane ever to land there?
3. The Concorde is a supersonic airplane. It can fly at 2000 miles per hour. If it took off from Metro Airport, how long would it take to get to the following cities: Denver, Dallas, Miami, Los Angeles, Mexico City, Moscow, Russia.
4. How have airplanes affected passenger travel on the railroads? Why?

Stage coaches in Michigan! Here's an ad dated 1854. (Michigan State Archives, History Division)

Chapter 12

Other Resources and Industries

Limestone — Coal — Salt — Oil — Gravel

Limestone. In an earlier unit you learned that for long periods of time all of Michigan, except the western part of the Upper Peninsula, was covered with water. In these ancient seas little marine animals, whose outlines can often be found in the limestone deposits today, once lived. When these small marine animals died their shells remained on the bottom of the ancient seas. Streams running down from the mountains brought lime and other minerals with them that also were deposited in the seas. Thus layer upon layer of calcium carbonate (calcite) and other minerals formed on the sea bottoms. As long periods of time passed, these shell remains, pieces of rock, and minerals were slowly pressed together to form sedimentary rock layers such as limestone or sandstone. These sea bottom deposits underlie all of the Lower Peninsula and the eastern part of the Upper Peninsula. In the Straits of Mackinac area and along the Detroit River some of the limestone rims of the underlying saucers come close to the surface of the land. Here it can be easily quarried and shipped in boats on the Great Lakes.

Much limestone is used in making cement. The BASF Wyandotte Corporation, at Wyandotte, uses limestone in manufacturing many of its products.

Much limestone is also used in smelting iron ore to make steel. About eight hundred pounds of limestone are used to make one ton of steel. Limestone is also used to make lime.

Limestone is taken from large open pit areas, called quarries, where the limestone is blasted from the Silurian or Devonian saucer rims. At Calcite, near Rogers City, is located one of the largest limestone quarries in the world. From this quarry comes much limestone that is used in making steel and in the chemical industries. At Port Inland, near Manistique, is a large limestone quarry. Most of the limestone quarried here goes to Chicago, Illinois, and Gary, Indiana, at the southern end of Lake Michigan where it is used for making steel. Dolomite is quarried at Port Dolomite, east of Cedarville. A dolomite quarry is also located on Drummond Island.

Alpena, Petoskey, Charlevoix, and Dundee also have large limestone quarries. Limestone from these quarries is used, along with gypsum and shale to make cement. Some limestone for making cement is shipped into southern Michigan from quarries in northern Ohio.

Coal. A medium grade of coal underlies part of the Lower Peninsula. It was formed during the Pennsylvanian Period, like the other world's deposits of coal, when this area was a large shallow swamp. Coal was first mined in Michigan in the mid 1830's near Jackson. Between 1860 and 1947 some forty-six million tons were mined. Peak production was reached in 1907 when 2,035,000 tons were marketed. In general, except near Saginaw, the coal veins are very thin. Mining was very expensive as the veins are covered by

not make good coke and is therefore useless for the steel industry. Neither is it good for making gas or heating homes. Because of these reasons Michigan's coal mines have not been in operation since 1946. Although much coal is used in Michigan for generating electricity all of it is shipped into the state from other areas. Coal boats run across Lake Erie nearly all winter long to bring coal to the Detroit area. Much

This is what the International Salt Company's Detroit mine looked like. For more than 75 years, huge equipment hauled salt under the streets of Detroit. The mine stopped production in 1982 but was open for tours for awhile.

glacial till. Much timbering had to be done to keep the glacial till from slipping and falling into the mines.

Michigan's coal is very soft and easily broken. Sulphur is found in it. It does

coal is shipped to ports on the upper lakes by boats. Some also comes into southern Michigan by unit trains direct from coal fields in other states.

Salt. Vast deposits of rock salt as well

as salt brines, found in sandstone, underlie most of the Lower Peninsula. During the Silurian Period much of the area was part of a large salty sea. As time passed and the water continued to evaporate, thick beds of rock salt formed. Above these salt beds layers of dolomite and shale formed. These layers of rock have kept water from seeping downward and carrying the salt away.

During the Mississippian Period salt brine formed in the porous rock laid down during this time. This salt brine forms the basis for several industries in Michigan. If the salt is found as a brine it is pumped to the surface in its natural state. In other places water is pumped down into the sandstone having the salt deposit. The water then picks up the salt and it becomes a brine. The brine is then pumped to the surface.

No real attempt was made to produce salt until 1860. In that year the state of Michigan began paying ten cents bounty for each bushel of salt produced as an aid to developing the new salt industry. Several sawmills, in the Saginaw Valley, began to burn their waste wood to evaporate the water from salt brine and get salt.

Since 1880, Michigan has been one of the leading salt producing states of the country. Salt brines are produced at Ludington, Manistee, Port Huron, St. Clair, and Midland. The Hooker Chemical Company at Montague, the Dow Chemical Company at Midland, the Morton-Norwich Company at Manistee and Port Huron, the Diamond Salt Company at St. Clair, and the BASF Wyandotte Corporation at Wyandotte, all use salt brine as the basis for many products.

Michigan had one salt mine where rock salt was blasted from an underground salt layer. It was located in southwestern Detroit. An elevator carried miners 1,135 feet down to salt layers which were nearly thirty feet thick. Some rock salt was used to keep streets and highways free of ice and snow in winter. Most of it was used in industry. This mine stopped production in 1982.

Oil. Early settlers found escaping oil and gas in Montcalm and Wayne counties. Sometimes the oil film on the water was so thick that cattle and horses refused to drink. In some places gas escaped in large enough amounts to be lighted.

As the glacial till covering Michigan varies from a few inches to hundreds of feet in thickness, it is difficult to find where oil pockets lie in the underlying rocks. Careful records have been kept of what materials have been found when wells have been drilled. From these records much has been learned about the rocks that lie under Michigan's glacial till.

Oil was first discovered at Port Huron in 1896. Since that time, oil has been found in many places in the Lower Peninsula: near Saginaw, Muskegon, Mt. Pleasant, Midland and Jonesville. A new field has been recently discovered in the northern part of the Lower Peninsula from Manistee to Traverse City and then across the state to Rogers City. Both oil and natural gas have been found in this area. They are now Michigan's most valuable natural resources as there is an increased demand for them.

Gypsum. Another mineral, similar to salt, is gypsum. A large saucer layer of gypsum lies under part of the Lower Peninsula. It outcrops in Kent and Iosco counties. Gypsum is used to make plaster of Paris, plaster, plaster board and wall board. The deposit of gypsum at Alabaster in Iosco County contains enough gypsum for many years. It is quarried here by the United States Gypsum Company and the National Gypsum Company. At Grand Rapids the gypsum is mined also.

Other Resources. Sand and gravel, deposited here by the glaciers, are also valuable resources for Michigan. Each year about 50 million tons of gravel are taken from gravel pits and used in mixing concrete, as ballast for railroad tracks, and making secondary roads. Sand for casting molds is shipped from Muskegon. Glass sand is quarried in Monroe County. Near Huron Bay on Lake Superior deposits of slate are found but they have not been worked for many years. From quarries at Grindstone City in Huron County, Marshall sandstone was quarried to make grindstones and whetstones for over one hun-

On hand-turned grindstones like this one the early settlers and lumbermen sharpened their tools.

dred years but the stone is no longer used.

In some parts of Michigan there are deposits of clay. Brick making was one of Michigan's earliest industries. Some clay tile is still made.

Michigan has developed some water power. Dams are located on several rivers in the Lower Peninsula and on rivers in the western part of the Upper Peninsula. At the dams, water power is used to generate electricity. From the power houses at the dams electricity is carried by high power transmission lines to many cities, villages and rural areas.

How Well Did You Read?

1. How was limestone formed?

2. Why is there much limestone under most of Michigan?

3. For what is limestone used?

4. Where are some of the large limestone quarries located?

5. During which geological periods were large deposits of limestone formed in the Michigan Basin?

6. How is most of the limestone shipped? Can you tell why?

7. During which geological period was Michigan's coal formed?

8. Why is coal no longer mined in Michigan?

9. During which geological periods were thick layers of salt deposits deposited?

10. In what two forms is salt found in Michigan?

11. Where is Michigan's only salt mine located?

12. Why is it difficult to locate oil pockets in Michigan?

13. Where is gypsum found? For what is it used?

14. From what material are bricks made?

15. Why have dams been built across some of Michigan's rivers?

Things to Do and Talk About

1. What can you find out about Grindstone City? Why are grindstones no longer made from sandstone? See p. 35 in **Vanishing Landscape** for information on millstones.

2. Be able to locate these places on a map of Michigan: Rogers City, Port Inland, Port Dolomite, Drummond Island, Petoskey, Charlevoix, Alpena, Saginaw, Jackson, Alabaster, Grand Rapids, Grindstone City, Ludington, Manistee, Mt. Pleasant, Port Huron and Montague. Now locate them on your outline map.

3. Be able to locate the following rivers on a map of Michigan: Au Sable, Manistee, Muskegon, Kalamazoo, Menominee, Thornapple, Tobacco, Saginaw, Grand and Rifle.

4. To find out more about the salt industry in Michigan read the article in the **Michigan History** magazine, page 16, January-February, 1981. (Volume 65, No. 1)

Recreation and Other Resources

Recreation. One of Michigan's greatest resources is the use of the area as a "Vacation Land" especially the area north of Clare and Bay City. Among the beautiful lakes, fast flowing streams and the lush green forests, many people find pleasant places to spend their vacations.

Today expressways and even airplanes make it easy for people to reach a favorite spot on some stream or lake. Many people living in the southern part of the state vacation or picnic at nearby lakes or go north to spend their vacations during the summer. Hundreds of others from Ohio, Indiana, and Illinois also vacation in Michigan or in other

Michigan's Tourist Attractions

-a selection of many in the state-

Isle Royale

Fort Wilkins

Copper Mines

Quincy Mine Hoist

Porcupine Mountains

Iron Industry Museum

Pictured Rocks

Tahquamenon Falls

Marquette

Soo Locks

S.S. Valley Camp

Sault Ste. Marie

St. Ignace

Mackinac Island

Fort Michilmackinac

Escanaba

Presque Isle lighthouse

Fayette Townsite

Boyne Mountain

Alpena

Jesse Besser Museum

Menominee

Sleeping Bear Dunes

Hartwick Pines

Traverse City

Higgins Lake

Houghton Lake

White Pine Village

Midland

Mt. Pleasant

Fremont

Bay City

Hackley House

Saginaw

Muskegon

Frankenmuth

Crossroads Village

Grand Rapids

Flint

Port Huron

Holland

Gerald Ford Museum

Dossin Great Lakes
Museum

S.S. Keewatin

Lansing

Pontiac

State Capitol

Detroit Zoo

Cranbrook Institute
of Science

Battle Creek

Ann Arbor

Detroit

Kalamazoo

Benton Harbor

Jackson

Renaissance Center

St. Joseph

Fort Wayne

Irish Hills

Henry Ford Museum

Greenfield Village

© Hillsdale Educational Publishers

Kalamazoo Aviation Museum

Boblo Island

Michigan Space Center

128

areas around the Great Lakes. Michigan ranks as one of the leading tourist states and the tourist industry is one of her largest industries and employs hundreds of people.

In Michigan visitors can see pretty waterfalls that are found in the western part of the Upper Peninsula. East of Munising, along the south shore of Lake Superior, lie the pretty Pictured Rocks formed of Cambrian sandstone. Many islands like Belle Isle, Mackinac Island, Beaver Island, Grand Island and Isle Royale are visited by hundreds of people every year.

Crack! Bang! or put..put..put.. wheeze. Would you like to know where you can see men in Revolutionary War uniforms practicing with their flintlocks or even cannon, or see antique cars putting along being driven by folks dressed in old fashioned clothes? Well, events featuring these things are just a few of the special summer activities that take place at Greenfield Village in Dearborn. The village is just one of many truly exciting places in our state to visit. Michigan has adventure and wonder to offer in many packages for those who will only look for it!

For example—In the southern Michigan town of Colon there is a magic convention each year to which several hundred magicians and visitors come.

In June or July of each summer, a hang gliding festival is held in Frankfort, Michigan. The gliders cast off from the high sand dunes and soar over Lake Michigan.

Honor, Michigan, hosts a Coho fishing festival in the early fall. These big fish can really put up a fight!

If you don't know what maple sugar is, then go to the maple sugaring week-end at the Nature Center in Kalamazoo held the second week in March.

Yachts race from Port Huron to Mackinac each July. It is a glorious sight to see the boats with their wildly colored sails dancing across the water.

If the roar of the snowmobile engines fascinates you, travel to Alpena or Sault Ste. Marie in January or February. They have two great snowmobile races. These races are known as The Thunder Bay 250 and the International 500.

Perhaps the Ski Flying Tournament near Bessemer is what you want to try! No matter what type of exciting time you want, you can find it in Michigan—just look!

"Tulip Time" in Holland, Michigan.

Many special events such as the "Blossom Festival" held each spring at St. Joseph, "Tulip Time" held each May in Holland, the "Cherry Festival" held each July at Traverse City, and "Bavarian Week" held each June at Frankenmuth are attended by many people.

When fall comes the green hills of summer gradually change to yellows, reds and browns as the leaves of the trees change to their bright fall colors. Then many people visit northern Michigan to see the fall colors. As the season moves on toward winter, hunters using bow and arrow come to hunt deer. These are followed by many others who visit the area to hunt for birds, bear, and deer.

Winter snows seldom block Michigan's highways and people come north to ski, toboggan, snowshoe, and ride through the woods on the new snowmobiles that have become so popular.

Fishing. Until a few years ago commercial fishing on the Great Lakes was one of Michigan's major industries. Whitefish, Mackinaw trout, sturgeon, pickerel and herring were caught and shipped in large amounts. The fishing industry employed hundreds of men. As late as 1940 the catch was a little over twenty-six million pounds and valued at over two million dollars. But during the meantime most of the commercial fishing has stopped. There are perhaps as many pounds of fish in the Great Lakes as ever but the fish are mostly what are called trash fish and have little value on the market. They are used for cat food and food for animals on fur farms.

During the 1920s sea lampreys made their way into the Upper Lakes from Lake Ontario by coming through the Welland Canal. Spreading eastward across Lake Erie they went up the Detroit and St. Clair rivers into Lake Huron and from there into Lake Michigan and Lake Superior.

Adult lampreys lay their eggs in streams flowing into the Great Lakes.

Larva and adult sea lamprey. Photo, Mich. Dept. of Natural Resources.

There the young are hatched. After spending four or five years in the stream bottom the young lampreys go down the stream and into the Great Lakes. Because there is no natural enemy in the Great Lakes to reduce their number the lampreys soon increased to many thousands. As the number of lampreys increased, commercial fishing slowly declined. A lamprey attaches itself to a fish, usually on the side of the fish. Then the single lamprey, or more than one, kills the fish by feeding on the blood of the fish.

A poison that kills lampreys, but not fish, has been put into streams flowing into the Great Lakes and the number of lampreys has declined. This treatment has been quite successful in Lake Superior and commercial fish are again on the increase there. Streams flowing into Lake Huron and Lake Michigan have also been treated and the lamprey in these lakes has decreased in number.

A small fish of poor commercial value called the alewife has also entered the Great Lakes. There they increased to vast numbers. Because they feed on the eggs of perch and other commercial fish they did much to reduce the numbers of these fish in the Great Lakes. Coho and Chinook salmon that have been planted in the Great Lakes, feed on the alewife. This has done much during the last few years to reduce the number of alewife. Because of this, perch and other fish are again increasing in number.

For many years both the state and national governments have operated fish hatcheries where small fingerlings are hatched and raised. Then the fingerlings are planted in the Great Lakes and in the inland lakes and streams. The work of these hatcheries has done much to improve fishing in Michigan.

In 1966, fingerling Coho salmon were planted in the Platte and Manistee rivers by the Department of Natural Resources. Since that time other plantings have been made in several other streams. Coho salmon spend three years in the deep, cold water of the Great Lakes. Then they return to the stream in which they were hatched, or planted. There they spawn and then die. So far the Coho salmon have done well in the Great Lakes and seem to have reduced the amount of alewife in the lakes. Each fall when the Coho come into the streams to spawn hundreds of them are caught by fishermen. Others are taken by the Department of Natural Resources for the eggs which are then hatched in fish hatcheries and then the fingerlings are released into streams that flow into the Great Lakes.

Some Chinook salmon have also been planted in the Great Lakes. These fish grow to as large as thirty pounds or more. So far large catches of these fish have not been made.

Not only has Great Lake's fishing been reduced because of the sea lamprey and the alewife but also by the amount of waste materials that have been allowed to go into Michigan's streams and Great Lakes. Water pollution is one of our major ecological problems today. The water of Lake Erie has been heavily polluted because of sewage and industrial waste that has been allowed to drain into the lake. Lake Michigan, because of its limited drainage and the many industrial cities that are found along its shore line, is now also becoming a polluted body of water. One of the major wastes that is found in the waters of the Great Lakes is DDT that was used on orchards, lawns, and farmlands before its use was forbidden by the government. Another pollutant is mercury that has been allowed to go into rivers and lakes by industries. Lake Superior has the least pollution of any of the Great Lakes as there are fewer people living in the area and a limited amount of industries. Today, better sewage and industrial waste plants are being installed to reduce water pollution but much still remains to be done to purify the water in our streams and lakes to make them safe for fish and people.

To Check Your Reading

1. Can you tell why Michigan is one of the leading vacation states?
2. Where is the "Blossom Festival" held each spring?

Empire Mine Pit, Palmer, Michigan. Electric Shovel Loading Production Haulage Truck.

Courtesy, Cleveland-Cliffs Iron Company.

Almost all of the iron ore mined in Michigan today comes from low grade open pit mines. When the rock is blasted from the working face of the mine, it is taken to the grinders where it is ground into a fine powder. The iron ore is then collected from the ground material and processed into taconite pellets containing about 65% iron ore. This picture shows an electric shovel loading a haulage truck at the working face of the Empire Mine in Palmer, Michigan.

This picture shows part of the Hi-Calcium Quarry from which limestone is quarried. It is seven miles from the Port Inland where the limestone is shipped on Great Lakes carriers.

Courtesy, Inland Lime and Stone Company, Gulliver, Michigan.

Tilden Mine.

Courtesy, Cleveland-Cliffs Iron Company.

The Tilden Iron Mine is located about three miles south of Ishpeming on an iron ore deposit known as the Tilden Reserve. This is Michigan's newest iron mine. This mine produces about 4,000,000 gross tons of high-grade pellets each year.

The building of large cabin cruisers at the Chris-Craft Company.

Courtesy, Chris-Craft Company. (Michigan State Archives — History Division)

3. What festival is held at Holland each spring?

4. What festival is held at Traverse City each summer?

5. Why has commercial fishing declined on the Great Lakes during the past few years?

6. How have modern highways helped the resort industry?

7. Why are Michigan's summers less warm than in some other places in the United States?

8. Where is Greenfield Village?

9. Name one summer and one winter festival or special event taking place in Michigan.

10. What kinds of salmon have been planted in the Great Lakes?

11. How have our streams, inland lakes and Great Lakes been polluted?

Things to Do and Talk About

1. On a map of Michigan locate the islands mentioned in this section.

2. Why is it easier to get to the northern part of the state today than it was thirty years ago?

3. What is being done in your area to combat water pollution? What else can be done by the people where you live?

4. Look in the latest copy of the **Michigan Natural Resources Magazine** for their calendar of events, or use the **Michigan AAA Magazine,** and list four events taking place for that month.

Other Industries

Furniture. As settlers came to Michigan there developed a need for furniture to furnish their homes. Woodworking craftsmen began to use pine and hardwood to make chairs, tables and other pieces of furniture. From this early beginning the furniture industry grew. Furniture has been made at many places in Michigan but gradually the city of Grand Rapids became, and still is, the furniture center in Michigan.

About 1840 a craftsman named William Haldane began making furniture at Grand Rapids. Soon other cabinet makers were also making furniture in the growing city and Grand Rapids became known as the "Furniture City." Here and in other places in Michigan a group of artisans with their original designs and skilled craftsmanship, make furniture of high quality.

At first, pine and hardwood from Michigan's forests were used but as choice wood became scarce furniture makers turned to other woods. Costly woods were brought from foreign lands and made into veneer and used to cover other wood to give beauty to furniture. Today there are several furniture factories in Grand Rapids area and a few are located in other cities.

Although wood is still used for making furniture, much furniture is now made of metal; such as filing cases, desks and desk chairs, chairs and tables. Michigan is a large producer of school, church and auditorium furniture. The leading centers in Michigan today are Grand Rapids, Menominee, Monroe and Holland.

Medicines. Before 1860 many people gathered herbs each fall that they used to make medicine in case of illness in the family. These herbs were used to make a brew which the ill person drank. Some remedies were brought here by the settlers and others were learned from the Indians. Just how strong these brews were no one knew. But after 1860 a few companies began to make one or two preparations that had a standard strength so that a doctor would know how much medicine he was giving a patient. Some of these early companies started here in Michigan.

Parke, Davis and Company in Detroit, the Upjohn Company in Kalamazoo, and the Dow Chemical Company in Midland are the largest producers of medicine but smaller ones also are located in the state. Here chemicals are carefully prepared into medicines, or for experiments, in their laboratories. From these experiments come many new preparations that have cured diseases in both people and animals. Most of the medicines used today have been developed since 1940.

Heating Units. In the early 1860's iron stoves began to replace fireplaces as a means of heating and cooking. In 1864 Jeremiah Dwyer and his brother began making stoves in a little foundry in Detroit. The Dwyer brothers not only made their stoves but

sold them as well. People liked the stoves because they gave more heat than the older fireplaces. Soon there were several stove companies in Detroit, and Detroit became known as the leading stove-producing city in the nation. Stoves were also made at Battle Creek and Kalamazoo.

These stoves were made of cast iron, with replaceable parts, and fancy nickel trim. Many kinds of stoves were made —ones for heating living rooms, cook stoves called kitchen ranges, hard coal burners, soft coal stoves, gas burning stoves, and even stoves that burned blubber for the Eskimos.

As the years have passed stoves have been replaced by newer and better heating units. Today there are many companies located in the cities of the southern part of the state that make heating equipment; such as oil burners, gas burners, fans, furnaces, boilers, safety valves, thermostats and air conditioners.

During the last few years, as natural gas and petroleum products have become more expensive, many people are again turning to stoves as a source of heat for keeping their homes warm. Farmers cut wood from their wood lots while people living in northern Michigan can secure a permit from the Department of Natural Resources to cut some kinds of wood in the state forests.

The Iron and Steel Industries. Although Michigan was the main source of iron ore up to 1890, most of the ore passed Detroit and went to the ore ports on the south shore of Lake Erie.

Michigan's first pioneer in the steel industry was Captain Ward. In 1853 he started the Eureka Iron and Steel Company at Wyandotte. This company had a blast furnace and rolling mill.

In those days only small amounts of steel were made and it was expensive. Steel is iron with the proper amount of carbon. Men at that time were experimenting to learn how larger and cheaper amounts of steel could be produced. One of these men was William Kelly. Mr. Kelly did some of his experimenting in Kentucky and then at Mr. Ward's mill at Wyandotte. Mr. Kelly discovered about 1850 (about the time that Mr. Bessemer discovered it in England) that if air was blown through the molten metal the carbon and other unwanted minerals would be burned from it. Once these impurities were removed the proper amount of carbon could be added to make steel of the desired quality. This was a big step ahead in the steel industry, and before long, several large steel mills were built in the eastern part of the United States.

In 1864 the plant at Wyandotte installed one of the first Bessemer furnaces, and it was at this plant that the first Bessemer steel was made in the United States. Here also the first T rails for railroads were made. For a time it was the largest industry in the Detroit area but it stopped production in 1890. In 1893 a blast furnace and iron works was built in Hamtramck but it ceased operating in 1905.

Mr. Henry Ford was the first to again make steel in Michigan. The Ford plant now produces well over a million tons of steel each year. The Michigan Steel Corporation built a plant on the Ecorse River and began making steel in 1929. Since that time other steel companies have built plants along the Detroit River. Now Michigan has steel plants located from River Rouge to Trenton.

Some of these steel mills have the most modern equipment. But as large as these plants are, they produce only a part of the steel used in Michigan's industries.

The Automobile Industry. From the fine hardwoods some of Michigan's early craftsmen made two wheeled carts, wagons and buggies. One of the early centers for this carriage industry was Flint, and years before it became known for the making of automobiles it was known as the vehicle city.

Between 1890 and 1900 people became interested in new means of transportation. One of these new means was the new safety bicycle that had two wheels the same size. Many bicycles were made at Bay City. Before 1900 these new bicycles were being made for women as well as men. Many people, especially in the growing cities, rode bicycles to and from work. But by this time the combustion engine began to be developed enough for use and men saw in this engine, which would run on gasoline, a new means of transportation that would provide a faster and easier means of transportation than could be had by horse-drawn vehicles or bicycles.

As men searched for a better means of transportation they turned to three sources of power, electric batteries, steam engines, and the new gasoline motor. Steam-driven buggies had been built as early as 1860 but because of poor roads they proved of little use. In 1886, Mr. Ransom E. Olds built a steam-driven auto and drove it around Lansing. In that same year Mr. Olds and his father organized the oldest unit in the present General Motors Corporation, the Olds Gasoline Engine Works. In the early days of automobiles several steam-driven autos, such as the White, Stanley Steamer, and Locomobile appeared on the market but steam power was not the answer to a better means of transportation. One had to wait until the water boiled before the car could be driven and then the water in the boiler would be all gone after driving only a few miles. More water would then have to be secured and heated. What is more, in the wintertime the water had to be drained from the boiler to keep it from freezing.

Electric battery driven cars had the disadvantage of not being able to go far until the battery had to be recharged. Batteries ran down and often left the driver some distance from home. What was needed was a machine that carried its own source of power.

In France and Germany men had been working on an engine that ran on coal gas that exploded time after time in a cylinder. A better source of power was soon to be found in gasoline. Refineries had been making kerosene for use in lamps and lanterns. While the petroleum was being heated to make kerosene it gave off a gas that was very explosive. Men soon found that this gas, now called gasoline, could be used to power the newly developing combustion engines and gasoline was cheap and plentiful. Here was a source of power that seemed to be needed in order to drive the new autos.

Many men began experimenting with the new gasoline engine and putting it in carriages and wagons. In 1894, Mr. Ransom E. Olds built a gasoline-driven auto and began driving it around Lansing. In 1895, Mr. Olds began to produce cars for sale. His Curved Dash Runabout was one of the most successful and popular cars at that time.

In 1896, Mr. Henry Ford built his first car. It was five feet in length. For wheels Mr. Ford used bicycle wheels. The car had two speeds—one forward and one backward. In 1898, the spark plug was invented by a Michigan lumberman named Frank W. Canfield. This was a great advance in the development of the gasoline engine because one could now regulate the time when the gasoline would explode in the cylinder. By 1899, there were twenty-five companies making automobiles in Michigan. But automobiles were expensive and there were then no good roads on which to drive.

In 1902, the oldest automobile company, still making automobiles in Detroit, was formed. It is now the Cadillac Motor Car Company. In 1903, David Buick and Benjamin Briscoe formed the Buick Motor Car Company, at Flint. In that same year the present Ford Motor Company was started. Many of the early car manufacturers made only a few cars before they went out of business. Today, such automobile names as Reo, Auburn, Marmon, Winton, Earl, Maxwell, Oakland, Willis St. Clair, Paige, Carter Car, Randolph, Saxon, and Briscoe are no longer heard.

The first automobiles were usually little more than wagons or buggies with little one-cylinder engines under them. Some of them cranked on the side to start up. Most of them had a chain drive like a bicycle. The first ones were steered by a lever called a tiller. Usually they carried only two or four people. Roads were very poor and anyone who went far from the city in rainy weather was apt to get stuck in the mud. There were no gasoline stations or garages.

Every car buyer had to be his own mechanic.

But automobiles had come to stay and soon they got away from the wagon and buggy look. Cloth tops, similar to buggy tops were added. Side curtains were made to put on, in case it rained. More cylinders were added and the motor was placed in the front of the automobile. At first, all the cars were cranked by hand but later self-starters were made. Some of the early cars were large and very expensive to buy, costing almost as much as a house!

However, some manufacturers, like Mr. Olds and Mr. Ford, saw a large market for cars if they could be made so that the common man could afford to own one. One of the best remembered of these early cars was the Model T that was first made by the Ford Motor Company in 1908. It was strong and light and had a motor of four cylinders. Because in the United States all traffic keeps to the right, car makers about this time changed the steering wheel to the left side of the car.

In 1908, The Fisher Body Corporation was organized. In 1909, the first Chevrolet car was made. In 1914, the first Dodge cars were made. In that year the Cadillac Motor Company came out with the first V-eight high speed motor. For some time Mr. Ford made his Model T cars in his large plant in Highland Park, but in 1915 he began building what is now the well-known River Rouge Plant, in Dearborn, to make Eagle boats to help win World War I. Later this plant became the main plant of the Ford Motor Company.

In 1908, General Motors Company was started. This company was a combination of several earlier automobile companies, such as Buick, Olds, Oakland, Cadillac, and various producers of auto parts. It became General Motors Corporation in 1916. Chevrolet was added to the group in 1918 and the Fisher Body Company in 1919.

The first Chrysler car was made in 1924. This corporation purchased the Dodge plant and continued making Dodge cars.

By this time only a few of the many companies that had started making automobiles were still in production. Though the number of companies was smaller, the number of cars leaving the assembly lines was growing larger and larger. On May 26, 1927, the fifteen millionth Model T left the assembly line. It was one of the last Model T's made. In December of that year, the Ford Model A began to be made. In December 1935 the eleven millionth Chevrolet car came off the assembly line.

As more and more cars were made there developed a demand for better roads on which to drive them. In 1905, the Michigan State Highway Department was started and since that time much has been done to build good roads in Michigan.

Today, Detroit, Flint, Saginaw, Lansing, and Pontiac are all centers making autos or auto parts. Hundreds of small plants in the state make standard parts for the assembly lines in the automobile plants.

Other Industries. The automobile industry is one of Michigan's best known industries, but let's not forget several of the other products made in our state.

As early as 1876, hand pushed carpet sweepers, having a central rotating brush, were made at Grand Rapids by

Melville R. Bissell. In 1909, vacuum cleaners began to be made in Detroit.

Just before 1900, breakfast foods began to be made at Battle Creek. At first they were made by several companies. Today, Battle Creek is known internationally for its production of breakfast cereals. General Mills, Post and Kellogg have large plants there.

General baking companies began marketing baked goods for sale in general stores and soon women were buying baked goods rather than baking them at home. Today there are several baking companies in Michigan.

Pulpwood, like this pile near Grand Marais, is now being cut in large amounts in Michigan. Pulpwood is used for making many paper products. Photo, 1967.

In 1920, the Burroughs Adding Machine Company started making adding machines in a plant at Detroit. This is now a large manufacturer of adding machines, calculators, computers and bookkeeping machines. This company now has plants in Plymouth and Ann Arbor.

Parts for refrigerators are made at Tecumseh. Gerber baby food is made at Fremont. The Wolverine World Wide Company at Rockford makes Hush Puppy shoes.

Several companies make computer systems, guidance control systems, data processing equipment and electrical control systems. The Lear Siegler, Inc. plant at Grand Rapids, is one of the largest companies in this field.

From Michigan's forests now comes a lot of pulpwood. This is made into paper at plants such as those at Monroe, Kalamazoo, Detroit, L'Anse, Munising, Ontonagon, Muskegon and Manistee. Hardboard is also made at other plants.

About eighty percent of all of Michigan's industry is located in the triangle formed by the Huron, Clinton and Detroit rivers in southeastern Michigan.

To Check Your Reading

1. What reasons can you give for the development of the furniture industry?
2. What city became known as the "Furniture City"?
3. What woods were used to make furniture?
4. How were medicines made in pioneer days?
5. Name some of the larger producers of medicines in Michigan today.
6. Where were stoves first made in Michigan? Why are wood stoves popular again?
7. Why did people like stoves better than fireplaces?
8. Who was Mr. Kelly and what did he do for the steel industry?
9. Where is steel now made in Michigan?
10. The automobile industry developed from what other industry?
11. What three kinds of power were used to run the early automobiles?

12. Who were some of the men who started to make automobiles?
13. What city is known for the making of breakfast foods?
14. What is the name of one of the first adding machine companies?
15. Where are the main automobile producing plants located in Michigan today?
16. In what part of the state are most of Michigan's industries located?
17. Name some places where paper is made.

Things to Do and Talk About

1. For more information about early cars look at **From Carriages to Cars** by Metcalf and **Tin Lizzie** by Peter Spier.
2. Find out how veneer is made. Why is it used and how?
3. Get a copy of the **Michigan Gift Guide** from the Michigan Dept. of Commerce, P.O. Box 30004, Lansing, MI 48909. Find out about all kinds of gift items made in Michigan.
4. What industries are located near your home? Why did they start there, was there a special reason?

Map Work

1. Write the following places in a column. Beside each city write something that is made there: Wyandotte, Grand Rapids, Flint, Lansing, Saginaw, Pontiac, Holland, Kalamazoo, Monroe, Highland Park, L'Anse, Muskegon, Manistee, Detroit, River Rouge, Trenton, Bay City, Battle Creek, Ann Arbor, Plymouth, Midland, Port Huron, Munising and Ontonagon.

Wouldn't this be fun! These fellows are testing early cars to see if they might make it through the Michigan winter.

(Clarke Historical Library, Central Michigan University)

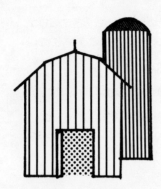

Chapter 13

Agriculture in Michigan

Factors That Influence Farming

Soil. All plants require soil in which to grow. Michigan's soil is what is called transplanted soil. It is glacial till that was brought south from Canada and left here by the glaciers when the ice melted. This glacial till setting on the underlying layers varies from a few inches in thickness to about six hundred feet in depth in the High Plains area in the north central part of the Lower Peninsula. Since the last glacier retreated north, weathering agents have done much to level the glacial till and sort out its various materials. Moraines, or hills as they are commonly called, have become lower and more rounded on the top as rain and running water have carried the finer materials, such as clay, into the valleys where outwash plains have formed. These plains often make good farm land. Streams also carried materials into the post glacial Great Lakes when they were higher than they are at present. Here the material settled to the bottom of the lakes. As the Great Lakes grew shallower, the edges of these former lake bottoms often became good farmland as in Wayne and Monroe counties and in the area south of Saginaw Bay. As plants, bushes and trees grew and died, their decaying debris added more humus to the soil.

In many areas forest fires have burned over the land. These fires often destroyed much of the humus that was in the soil before it was burned. Thus, much of its value was destroyed. Because of these forest fires much of Michigan's area, as in the High Plains area and the eastern part of the Upper Peninsula, is now not suited for good plant growth. Water falling on these areas runs away quickly or sinks into the ground. Thus, running water has carried away many of the necessary minerals and trace elements that are needed by growing plants and leaving only sand which has little value for plant growth. Some areas are clays that bake too hard in the summertime. Still other areas are swamp land and unsuited to farming. A few areas are muck land where decaying vegetation has slowly collected. Muck lands are good for growing some special crops. These different soils, together with varying amounts of rainfall and temperature limit farming to certain areas and crops. About one third of Michigan's land area is now classed as farm land. The rest is classed as land suited to the growing of trees and new forests now cover much of this area.

Rainfall. In order for plants to grow they require not only good soil but also rainfall and sunshine. This rainfall must come at the right time of the growing season. Michigan has an average rainfall of about 31 inches a year. This rainfall varies from about 28 inches in some areas, such as the Thumb, to about 36 inches in the south central and southwestern part of the state along the Michigan-Indiana boundary line.

Temperature. All plants must have enough frost free days to allow them to grow and ripen. The average annual temperature in Michigan varies from 49 degrees in the southern part of the state to 39 degrees in the northern part. The number of days free from frost varies from 180 days in the southwestern part of the state to about 90 days in Iron County in the Upper Peninsula, and Crawford County in the Lower Peninsula. In some parts of the state spring frosts may occur as late as the 10th of June. In Michigan the length of the growing season is affected by the latitude, elevation, and the effect of the Great Lakes, especially Lake Michigan, upon the temperature. Although the summer days are a little longer in the upper part of the state they are usually cooler and most plants do not grow as well there as they do in the southern part of the state.

How the Great Lakes Affect Michigan's Climate. The Great Lakes, that border Michigan on three sides, have much effect on Michigan's climate. This is especially true of Lake Michigan and the Lower Peninsula. During the summer months the water in Lake Michigan slowly warms. In the fall the prevailing winds, blowing in from the lake, keep the land area bordering the lake from warming and cooling as rapidly as it does inland. During October and November the lake is 15 to 20 degrees warmer than the land. Then the winds blowing in from the lake tend to warm the land. This gives the lake shore area some 20 to 30 more frost free days. During the early part of winter the winds, passing over Lake Michigan, warm and pick up moisture from the lake. As the winds come inland, across the cooler land, they cool and the moisture, squeezed from the cooling air, falls as snow. That is why the western part of the state, along Lake Michigan, receives a heavy snow fall during the early part of the winter. As water warms slower than the land, when spring comes the westerly winds, blowing in from Lake Michigan, tend to keep the land along the lake cool until the danger of frost has passed. This is one reason why the western part of the Lower Peninsula is a fruit growing area. Because of the prevailing westerly winds Lake Huron and Lake Superior have less effect than Lake Michigan on Michigan's agriculture.

Markets. A farmer must not only be able to grow crops but must have a market for his crops after they are raised. If the market is far away much of his profit is lost in paying the cost of transportation. Michigan's best farming areas, in general, are in the southern part of the Lower Peninsula. Here are found the best soils, the heaviest rainfall, and the longest growing season. Winters are shorter and less severe and thus less feed has to be stored to feed livestock during the winter months. Here also are ready markets for the crops that are grown. Most of Michigan's people live in this area. Cities; such as, Detroit, Muskegon, Grand Rapids, Saginaw, Bay City, Kalamazoo, Toledo, Ohio, and Chicago in Illinois, are close by and provide large markets for farm produce. The area is well supplied with good roads and railroads over which the produce can be quickly sent to market.

Can You Answer These?

1. What is the average temperature for the southern part of Michigan? for the northern part?
2. Which part of the state has the longest growing season? How long is it?
3. Which counties have the shortest growing season? Can you find these counties on a map of Michigan?
4. How does Lake Michigan affect Michigan's climate?
5. What is Michigan's average annual rainfall?
6. How much of Michigan's area is classed as farm land?
7. What factors influence farming?
8. How was much of Michigan's humus destroyed?
9. Why are close markets important to farmers?
10. Where are most of Michigan's best farm lands located?
11. How did the glaciers affect Michigan's soil?

Some Things to Do and Talk About

1. Try to find in your library, or geography book, a rainfall map of the United States. How does the rainfall of Michigan compare with other areas of the United States?
2. Where would you look in your newspaper to find out what kind of weather your community is expecting during the next few hours? Look up the weather for tomorrow.
3. How cold does it sometimes get in your community? How warm?
4. Keep a record of the temperature in your community for a month. Make your reading at the same time each day.
5. Find out what kind of soil is found near your home. Is it good for raising crops? Why?
6. How did the system of land survey affect the shape of Michigan's farms?

The Changing Farm Pattern

Michigan's First Farmers. The Indians were Michigan's first farmers. How they farmed, and what crops they raised, was told in the chapter on Indians. During the French and English periods the fur trade was the major occupation but a few farmers grew some crops in what is now Michigan.

142

Because of poor transportation there was only a limited market for their crops. Therefore, they grew only crops for their own and local use. Seeds and stock were low in quality and farming methods were very poor.

The Early Settlers. The opening of the Erie Canal made it possible for settlers to come to Michigan and for them to send their agricultural products to the growing markets in the cities of the East. Between 1825 and 1835, over 200,000 settlers came to Michigan to start farming on the new land. At first small fields began to be cleared in the forest. Later, as more land was cleared each year, larger fields, fenced by split rail or stump fences, replaced the forests that had for so long covered the land. These early settlers brought with them better grades of seed and stock that had been developed in the East. By 1860, the area south of Bay City was settled. In the period between 1860 and 1900 more farms were started on the cut-over lands in the northern part of the state. There the lumbering industries provided the farmers with a local market for their crops and employment during the wintertime. But farming north of Bay City was hindered because of the poorer soil, in most areas, and the colder climate. Since 1920, hundreds of these farms have been abandoned. Much of this land is now in state and national forests.

Changing Farming Methods. At first Michigan's farmers were general farmers. They kept a few cows, horses, hogs, and chickens and raised a variety of crops to supply the needs of their families and farm animals. Any extra crops were sold to get money to purchase the items they needed. But, before many years had passed some of them began raising what are known as cash crops. These are crops that can be sold on the market to bring in a cash return. One of the first of these cash crops was wheat. Wheat grew well on the land in southern Michigan. It did not easily spoil and could be sent to market on the Erie Canal, or the new railroads, and sold in the newly growing cities of the East or shipped on to markets in Europe. For many years Michigan was a leading wheat producer. Later other special crops; such as, potatoes, cherries, mint, celery, beans, and cucumbers for pickles, became major cash crops in certain areas. In fact, there are very few general farmers left in Michigan and their production is very small. Most farmers today specialize in one or two major crops.

Farming today is much different from what it was when the settlers first started farms in Michigan. Farmers then had none of the modern machines to help them do their work. Many of their common tools; such as, flails, pitchforks, rakes and harrows were homemade from wood from the nearby forest. Only small amounts of iron were used in making these tools during the days Michigan was being settled. Much of the farm work like planting, hoeing, harvesting the grain and threshing it, and milking the cows had to be done by the settlers and their families.

Soon after 1830, changes began to be made in the way farmers did their work. After the Bessemer steelmaking process made steel plentiful and inexpensive, tools made from steel began to replace the earlier ones made of wood and iron. Sickles, that had been used for hundreds of years to harvest grain, were replaced by scythes and these in turn by mowing machines pulled by a team of horses that cut the grain much faster. Threshing machines, powered by horses turning a sweep, were used to thresh the grain. Later these threshing machines were powered by steam engines called threshing engines. Steel plows replaced the earlier wooden ones. Windmills began to be used to pump water for the stock. Corn planters, better harrows, seed drills, twine binders, and cultivators made the farmers' work easier. These new machines also made it possible for them to produce larger crops and thus have more produce to sell to people who were living in the growing cities and working in the new industrial plants.

Before 1925, many draft horses were used on farms to pull plows, harrows, cultivators, mowing machines, and wagons. They were the farmers' main source of power. Draft horses, in Michigan, reached their largest number in 1917 when there were about 680,000 in the state. Today, there are only a few draft horses left on Michigan farms. When the gasoline engine was developed for automobiles some men began experimenting with a power machine that could be used by farmers to help them do their field work. Gasoline engines were placed in a new vehicle we now call a tractor. At first they were small and not very powerful but since 1925 tractors have become larger and more powerful.

Now powerful tractors provide the needed power for field work and farmers can do more work in a few minutes than a farmer, one hundred years ago, could do in a day. Electric power also aids farmers by running water pumps, milking machines, cooling tanks for milk, barn cleaners and heating units.

There were 206,960 farms in Michigan in 1910. There were a little over nineteen million acres in farm lands in 1920 and the average farm size was 97 acres. Since 1920, many farms have been abandoned and others have been added to present farms. Now there are about 78,000 and the average size is 177 acres.

Each year new machines are invented to help with the crops. Machines that replace men and women at harvest time are especially useful for the farmer. New devices have been developed to pick cucumbers and to shake ripe cherries out of the trees. Others help prepare sugar beets for harvest. Less migrant labor is needed now because of these machines. The Hispanic and Mexican people who often did this work have found better jobs in the cities. In the past these people did backbreaking work in the fields to help feed the state.

Can You Answer These?

1. Who were Michigan's first farmers?
2. What kind of fences did the early settlers use?
3. Why are there fewer farms north of Bay City?
4. How did the Erie Canal affect the settlement of Michigan?

5. What is meant by a general farm?

6. What are some of Michigan's special crops?

7. What were some of the changes in farming over the years?

8. Why are horses no longer used for farm work?

9. Why are there fewer farms in Michigan today than there were in 1910?

10. Who are migrant workers?

Things to Do and Talk About

1. To learn more about crops grown in Michigan, have a class member write for **Michigan Food and Fiber Facts** from the Michigan Dept. of Agriculture, Communications Division, P.O. Box 30017, Lansing, MI 48909.

2. If someone you know takes the **Michigan Farmer** bring a copy of it to class.

3. Can you find pictures of some of the modern farm machinery? Check with a farm equipment dealer — maybe he could give you some advertising materials.

Some Michigan Crops

A variety of agricultural products are produced in Michigan. It has many more crops than most of the states. This is possible because of the varied climate and soil conditions.

Dairy farming is very important, and dairy products have the largest dollar value making up about 27% of the total farm income. Grain is the next largest farm product representing about 17%. Beef cattle produce about 13.5% of the farm sales.

Dairy products are produced generally in all areas of Michigan. Over the last twenty years there has been some reduction in the number of dairy cows, probably due to the greater cost of equipment and feed. Southcentral Lower Peninsula is the area which has the most dollar value of dairy products. As shown by the following list, milk has a greater volume of production than other dairy products.

Dairy production for a recent year:
    5,250,000,000 pounds of milk
        55,054,000 pounds of butter
        35,774,000 pounds of cheese
        33,475,000 gallons of ice cream

Saginaw, Bay, Monroe and Lenawee counties in the southern part of Michigan have the highest value of grain production.

Our state was once a leading wheat producer, but the Michigan market started to fall in the 1890's as more wheat was grown in the plains states of the West. Most Michigan wheat is winter wheat which means it is planted in the fall, survives the winter, and is ready to be cut the next summer. This is not the way most crops are planted.

Michigan Agricultural Products
Main Products For Each County

Michigan is among the top ten producers in the U.S. of 45 agricultural products which range from navy beans to Christmas trees. Recently we ranked first in:

blueberries, eastern soft white winter wheat, navy beans, plantation Christmas trees, cucumbers and red tart cherries.

Oats, barley and rye are three other grains grown here. Oats is a softer grain that is fed to horses because it is easier for them to eat than wheat. More oats were grown in earlier times when horse-power was used on farms and cities. Corn is another of Michigan's grain crops. You will most likely see corn growing in the southern Lower Peninsula. This part of Michigan is on the northern edge of what is known as the corn belt. This belt is the area where most of America's corn is grown, and it reaches from Ohio across Iowa. We eat sweet corn, but another kind is field corn which is fed to cattle, chickens and pigs. Most of our corn is the field corn variety. Corn stalks are not wasted, but are cut up and made into silage for cattle feed too. Michigan farmers also grow some popcorn.

The crop of soybeans is a farm item that is seldom seen on anyone's table at supper time. This crop is used as a stock feed and to give soybean oil which is used in cooking and in several industrial products including plastics. Lenawee and Monroe counties are the leading soybean growers.

In the area of the Lower Peninsula next to Lake Michigan, the climate is very good for raising certain fruits. Plums, peaches, apples, grapes and cherries are specialties of this part of the state. The Traverse City region is a real cherry grower. Nearly three-fourths of all the tart cherries grown in the United States come from here. Well over 50,000 tons are produced in most years.

Moving toward the southern end of Lake Michigan, grapes are grown especially in Berrien and Van Buren counties. Grapes are made into juice,

jam, jelly and into wine. A large wine industry is located in this part of our state.

Throughout the state, strawberries, blueberries and apples are grown. Michigan is one of the top three apple growing states. So much fruit is grown in the southwestern part of the state that the largest non-citrus fruit market in the United States is located in Benton Harbor. Many canneries are located in the fruit producing areas of the state.

The raising of beef cattle is another important part of our agricultural business. Recently, there were about 548,000 cattle on Michigan farms. The number raised for beef changes due to the prices paid to farmers. When meat prices are high, it is usually because there are not so many cattle available for sale. When farmers see higher prices, they then raise more cattle. After a while, the prices tend to fall because more cattle can be sold. This is called the principle of supply and demand.

Pigs (hogs) and sheep are some other animals often seen on farms, though they are not usually a farmer's main income. Sheep give us wool as well as meat (mutton).

Poultry, mostly chickens, but also some turkeys, ducks and geese are raised here. Today, there are large chicken farms which are almost like factories where chickens are kept inside long low buildings, and the eggs are collected on conveyor belts. Over a billion eggs are produced each year.

Michigan farmers raise a wide variety of vegetables on their farms. Some people specialize in one or two vegetables, while others grow many kinds. Small farmers often open roadside stands and sell their vegetables to people who drive by.

Cucumbers are made into pickles, and Michigan ranks as the biggest cucumber grower in the United States. Almost 130,000 tons are produced each year.

Michigan also leads the nation in growing dry, edible beans. Navy beans are grown in really large amounts on farms near Saginaw. About 450 million pounds of dry beans are produced each year. We have so many that we export them by sea to other countries.

A sampling of some other Michigan vegetable crops are asparagus, celery, carrots, tomatoes, potatoes (especially in the western part of the Upper Peninsula), red beets, cabbage, leaf lettuce, peas, squash, pumpkins and melons.

Besides red beets, a valuable and useful beet grown in Michigan is the sugar beet. It is a very large white beet that contains about 20% sugar. This sugar can be concentrated, purified and cry-

stalized and is just like sugar from sugar cane. These beets are grown in the Saginaw River Valley-Thumb area. We produce almost 1.5 million tons of sugar from these beets. That is a lot of sugar!

Michigan people harvest some rather special things for food. Among these are peppermint and spearmint used for flavoring; maple syrup, for pancakes and waffles, which comes from the sap of maple trees; honey from bees; sunflower seeds for people and bird feed.

We are lucky to have so many good foods growing in our state for us to eat —we even have spinach!

Remember the important things which control what is grown in a certain place are (1) climate, including length of growing season, (2) soil type, and (3) nearness of the farm to the consumer and the number of consumers to buy the food.

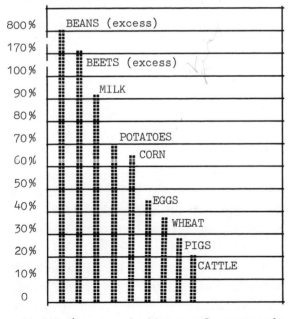

MICHIGAN'S FARM PRODUCTION
VERSUS MICHIGAN'S NEEDS FOR EACH CROP

800% BEANS (excess)
170%
100% BEETS (excess)
90% MILK
80%
70% POTATOES
60% CORN
50%
40% EGGS
30% WHEAT
20% PIGS
10% CATTLE
0

At 100 % our production equals our needs

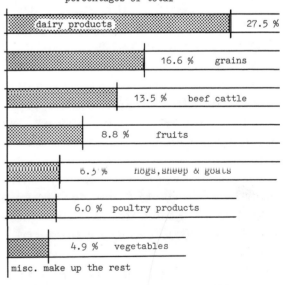

MICHIGAN'S MAJOR AGRICULTURAL PRODUCTS
percentages of total

dairy products — 27.5 %
16.6 % grains
13.5 % beef cattle
8.8 % fruits
6.3 % hogs, sheep & goats
6.0 % poultry products
4.9 % vegetables
misc. make up the rest

Check Your Reading

1. What is the type of product produced in Michigan that has the largest value?

2. In what section of the state is fruit widely grown?

3. What is the main farm product in your county?

4. What kind of wheat is usually grown here?

5. List things that determine what type of crops that are grown in certain areas.

6. Which crop do we produce in the greatest excess over our needs.

Some Things to Talk About and Do

1. Collect samples of several crops and show them to the class, examine them and be able to identify major ones like: wheat, oats, sugar beets, navy beans, soy beans, etc.

2. From reliable sources determine the current price for various grains, fruits and vegetables especially products grown in your area.

3. In the early mining days miners carried their lunches into the mines. Often they ate a meat and vegetable pie called a pasty. An article telling more about this can be found in **The Chronicle,** page 12, Spring, 1980.

Chapter 14

Michigan's People

Michigan is a great state. Its land, minerals, forests and farms helped to make it so, but the real thing that makes it great is its people. People are going to keep our state great with their ideas, inventions and hard work.

Michigan was once covered by forests, and only a handful of people made their homes here. It may have been a prettier state then, but not much was happening here. It wasn't until the people came, that dynamic changes started to take place.

Pioneers traveled to Michigan for adventure, for challenge, for freedom, for a chance to make money and an opportunity to try to make their dreams come true. Some succeeded, and others have not; but their lives and attempts add the real character to our history.

You know that the French arrived first and lived and worked with the Indians. Later, the English moved in and began to wrestle the land from these first Michigan people.

In the early days before the Erie Canal, not many people knew what Michigan had to offer, and so few moved here. Later, they realized that there was good farm land here—land that they could own themselves and be free to work without others telling them what they had to do. This is something most Americans have always wanted.

Farmers from New York state found that their farm land was not growing as much as it once did. (They did not know much about fertilizers then.) Some wanted more adventure and a change of life; so, they packed up their families and took the Erie Canal west, probably finishing the trip on a Lake Erie steamboat landing at Detroit.

People from the northeastern states suddenly began to arrive here in large numbers during the 1830's. Michigan had less than 30,000 people living here in 1830, but by 1840, there were 212,-267. The newcomers settled mostly in the counties near Detroit. At that time it was really tough to go any farther because of the poor roads and the limited transportation provided by the few trains.

Most of our first rush of settlers were from other states and not foreign born. There were French people left over from our days as a part of France though, and many spoke French. There were even some French newspapers.

Life certainly was not easy for any of the new Michiganders, but we were growing. Soon, there was a need for people to mine copper and iron, build canals and roads, and sail the ships. Most of the first settlers were farmers and often did not have skills to do such things. To get people to do this work, men were hired in Europe and brought to Michigan. Others heard of jobs here and came on their own. These men were good at their jobs and knew what to do, but they were strangers in the new land speaking a different language. Because of this, they often stayed together with others from their own country. They did not want to feel lonely. They wanted to be able to talk to friends and to eat the same kind of food as they had, play the same games in their free time, and to worship in the same kind of church.

People moved to Michigan from Germany, Holland, Norway, Sweden, Switzerland, Finland, France, England and Canada. There were also still Indians living in some places. There were some blacks who had escaped from slavery or had been freed by laws in some other states.

After the end of the Civil War, even more Europeans came here. They had their dreams, and many felt that once here, they could have their chance. They felt life in Europe was not right for them. They were being pushed around there. Political and religious ideas were changing, and these folk wanted the freedom of America. They heard they could actually own land, and there was land for sale in Michigan—and jobs! In Europe there was little cheap land; it was usually controlled by a large landowner. You could pay rent all your life, and not own anything. Here there were trees to cut and lumber to be sawed. Because our state was growing, people could work as store clerks, furniture makers, blacksmiths, barrel makers, railroad workers, sailors, fishermen, and much more.

The number of foreign born people living in Michigan increased constantly from the mid 1800's through the early 1900's. In 1880, about one in five had been born overseas.

Near the turn of the nineteenth century, more people came here from eastern and southern Europe. Polish, Russians, Italians, Greeks, Hungarians, and many more moved to Michigan. They found jobs in the many new factories that were starting here. There were jobs that were rather easy to do and did not require too much special training—just hard work—in the building of cars, steel making, stove construction or chemical production, etc. People also moved here from other states, while some of the people in Michigan left to go West.

Both world wars brought many blacks to Michigan from the south seeking higher paying jobs in factories making ships, tanks, and airplanes.

Even today people from other lands move to Michigan. People seeking a better life from Vietnam, Lebanon or Mexico, among other places, are growing in numbers.

All of these people have left their mark on our state. There are towns and cities with foreign names. Hamtramck near Detroit is a city with a Polish name. Customs and ideas were brought here. Foods too, are now a part of our heritage from the foreign settlers. One example is the pasty, a meat and vegetable pie, eaten by Cornish miners, and still served in the Upper Peninsula. Today, we have Greek, Lebanese and Arab restaurants; all brought here by new Michigan citizens from far away.

Now, it's time to find out more about the special people who make Michigan great. Not each person had a glorious career or earned a fortune, but many tried. Some did succeed, and many more are still working hard toward their own dreams today.

Over the years, there have been many famous and interesting people growing up or working in Michigan. Many of their names you will never have heard of. Their deeds are now forgotten except in history books. New people have come to take their places in the news.

Let's take some time to look back, re-discover and dust off the accounts of some of these men and women.

In the chapters of this book we have already talked about the French explorers who first came here. Cadillac is one to remember because he helped to start and govern Detroit, our largest city. Nicolet, LaSalle, Joliet were other explorers. Pere Marquette brought the Catholic religion here.

There were pioneers who came here before the land was cleared to start the first path of civilization. Women, as well as men, worked hard during those first years. Madame Cadillac was one of the first women. Susan Johnston was an Indian girl who married a white trader. She helped form some of the Indian treaties.

Let's not forget the Indians themselves. They knew how to live with nature and not destroy it. There were Indian leaders and heroes. Chief Pontiac was one of these. We do not know about many of them because there was no history written by Indians.

Henry Schoolcraft was a pioneer who did write down many Indian legends and information about the Indian way of life.

People were curious about this new state, and they wanted to know more about its resources. Douglass Houghton collected minerals and information about what the wild land held in the 1840's.

Lewis Cass and Stevens T. Mason helped to lead the people politically during the early years.

Crosswhite and his family fought for their freedom here to escape slavery. Sojourner Truth and other blacks, and whites too, helped to keep Michigan a place for the free at heart.

The state grew, and new ideas and inventions were developed here. Many dreamers wanted to see what they could do with these ideas. Henry Ford, Billy Durant, Nash, Dodge and others wanted to see what could be done with the car. They succeeded beyond anyone's wildest thoughts, and they gave our state its main industry.

Other men started new industries. Herbert Dow found new ways to get chemicals from salt brine and worked on ways to use Michigan's underground riches.

Kellogg and Post had a brainstorm and decided to make dry cereals that are seen on almost every breakfast table today.

Thomas Edison, one of our greatest inventors, worked here for a while when he was young.

Charles Lindbergh, who was the first to fly over the Atlantic Ocean, was born here and his father went to law school in Michigan.

Ralph Bunche was a famous black diplomat who was awarded the Nobel Peace Prize. He too came from Michigan.

Walter Reuther helped to start labor unions here. He wanted every man to be able to earn a good living and have a safe, healthy place to work, and the right to discuss his wages with business owners.

Even the "Lone Ranger" was born here—in a way. The first Lone Ranger character was from a Detroit radio program, before television.

There are many, many more great and exciting people who could be talked about from our past, but let's see what people we should know who are not quite so old.

Many of the people we hear about on the news are sports men and women playing in or from our state.

The early settlers of Michigan had little time or facilities to enjoy sports as we know them today. They did enjoy sports contests such as canoe racing, running, horseback riding, log splitting and rifle shooting. In the early nineteen hundreds the average man was working a twelve hour day, six days a week. It was unheard of for women to participate and enjoy sports such as they do today. Most of our modern sports were developed after 1900.

Today there are many different sports for both men and women to take part in or to watch. There are many professional sports in Michigan—sports in which men and women earn their living by playing or taking part. Each of these sports has an enthusiastic following of fans and favorite players.

In 1968 the Detroit Tiger baseball team was the talk of all Michigan when they won the American League Pennant and went on to win the World Series. A few of the favorite players of the winning team were Denny McLain, Bill Freehan, and Al Kaline. Kaline is now in the Baseball Hall of Fame. The Tigers won the World Series again in 1984.

The Detroit Lions football team now plays in the enclosed 'Silver Dome' stadium at Pontiac. Most home games are played before a capacity crowd of 80,000.

Professional basketball is a popular sport—the Detroit Pistons fans have their favorite players. Dave Bing and Bob Lanier were two of the outstanding players on the team. Ervin "Magic" Johnson from Lansing helped the Michigan State University team win the national championship. He now plays professionally.

In boxing, Detroit (and all of Michigan) had Joe Louis who was heavyweight champion of the world from 1937-1949. He was one of the most popular professional fighters and did much to advance the sport of boxing. Thomas Hearns is another nationally known boxer from Detroit.

The Detroit Red Wings, professional hockey team, have always provided sports fans with plenty of excitement. The Detroit team has won the Stanley Cup six times—1955 was the last time. Two of the popular players of a number of years ago were Gordie Howe and Sid Abel—both have been inducted into the Hockey Hall of Fame.

Each year more and more men and women of Michigan are playing golf. Michigan has its share of professional golf tournaments. Two of Michigan's professional golf players are Mike and Dave Hill of Jackson.

Tennis is one of the fastest growing sports in Michigan. In recent years many indoor courts have been built near cities in the state. A number of women from Michigan have joined the ranks of the women's professional tennis tour—one of the better known players is Rosemary Casals of Detroit.

Other professional sports in Michigan are horse racing, auto racing at Michigan International Speedway near Jackson,* soccer at Pontiac's Silverdome Stadium, skiing and ski jumping at Iron Mountain, snowmobile racing, power boat racing on the Detroit River, and the Detroit to Mackinac sailboat race. Other professional sports include bowling, ice skating, skeet and rifle shooting, etc.

How fortunate we are to live in Michigan where the many lakes, rivers, forests and parks make it possible to enjoy so many out-of-door sports. Many of these sports can be done by yourself or with your family—this type of sport could be hiking, back packing, bicycling, camping, canoeing, ice fishing, water skiing, and horseback riding.

Michigan has had many talented political leaders. G. Mennen Williams was governor for twelve years and also chief justice of the state supreme court. George Romney was governor in the 1960s. William Milliken was governor for fourteen years, more than anyone else. Martha Griffiths was a congresswoman for many years, and also served as lieutenant governor.

Gerald Ford from Grand Rapids was also in Congress representing Michigan

---

*Gordon Johncock of Indianapolis 500 fame is from Michigan.

before becoming President of the United States. His wife, Betty, is an interesting and outspoken person in her own right.

If you want to laugh, cry or be entertained, Michigan can help with that too! Here are some people born or bred here whom you should know: Tom Selleck from Magnum P.I.; Diana Ross, one of the original Supremes; Lily Tomlin, the comedian; singers Aretha Franklin, Bob Seger, Madonna, and Ted Nugent; and Oscar-winning composer and singer Stevie Wonder.

When the space age arrived, Michigan people were ready for it. Roger Chaffee was testing the Apollo capsule when he and two others were killed in a fire. James McDivitt from Jackson flew into outer space twice—once with Edward White who made our first space walk, and again with Apollo 9, the first flight of the lunar capsule.

As more history is written, people from Michigan will be included with their stories and accomplishments.

You are the future, and what you work to become, and what you succeed at will shape the state of Michigan tomorrow.

Check Your Reading

1. Give a few reasons why early settlers wanted to come to Michigan.

2. From what part of the country did many early settlers come from?

3. During what period of time did the boom of new pioneers start coming to Michigan?

4. Name 5 other countries that many people came from to Michigan.

5. List 5 important people who have lived here. Tell what they are famous for.

Things to Do

1. Trace your family heritage, What foreign countries are your ancestors from. What would you say the major nationality of your family is?

2. Make a list of each person in the class with the main nationality of their family. Which country is listed the most?

The city of Detroit skyline as seen from across the Detroit River in Windsor, Ontario. (Photo - August, 1976)

Courtesy, Harry J. Wolf

Glossary

Acetylene (ah SET i leen) A flammable gas that once was used for lighting in houses, cars, and mines.

Adze (ADZ) A cutting tool like an axe, except the blade is at right angles to the handle, like the blade of a hoe.

Allot, alloted. To set aside. Can refer to land, such as an Indian reservation.

Archeologists (ar key OL o jists) Scientists and historians who study the past by looking at things left behind by earlier people.

Artifacts (AR ti facts) A man-made object; usually something buried or lost, and then found by an archeologist.

Auger (AHG er) A hand tool for boring holes, made of a metal drill and a handle.

Bail Money given to the court or police when a suspect is released to make sure he or she will not run away. If he does, the money is kept by the court.

Bellows (BELL ohz) A device which will blow air when it is squeezed together.

Beneficiation (ben if ish ee AY shun) A process of making something more pure.

Blooms Large pieces of cast metal usually weighing several hundred pounds, often in the form of a bar.

Bobsleigh (BOB slay) A short sled, usually hooked together in two parts like train cars. They turn more easily because they bend where they are hooked together.

Boiler A device for making steam by heating water; the steam can be used to run different kinds of steam engines.

Boom A line of connected floating timbers across a river or any body of water. It keeps logs for a sawmill from floating away.

Brine A solution of salt in water. Other chemicals are often present as well.

Calk, calked (KAWK) To put metal studs or plates on the bottom of boots, horseshoes, etc. to give better traction.

Cambrian (KAM bree an) A geological time period millions of years ago when life is thought to have existed only in the seas.

Canals (ka NALS) Man-made riverways or waterways usually used for small boats.

Carbide (KAR bide) A rock-like chemical that fizzes when mixed with water, giving off acetylene.

Chert An impure flintlike rock, usually dark in color.

Cobbler (KOB ler) A person who makes or fixes shoes.

Conspiracy (kon SPEAR ah see) A plan by several people usually to do something illegal.

Cooper A person who makes or repairs wooden barrels.

Copper sulphide (SUL fide) A chemical made from copper and sulphur. It is black and does not dissolve in water.

Cords Amounts of wood, usually wood cut for a stove or fireplace. A cord is 8 feet long, 4 feet high, and 4 feet wide.

Cultivator (KUL ti vay ter) A farm tool that loosens soil and rakes up weeds when it is pulled between rows of growing plants.

Deciduous (dee SID you us) A term to describe trees which lose their leaves in autumn.

Decking ground A loading area on a railroad line where logs are loaded on flatcars.

Devonian (dee VOH nee an) A geological period noted for rapid development of life on land such as insects, plants, and animals with backbones.

Dolomite (DOL o mite) A rock made of calcium, magnesium, and carbon dioxide.

Dredge (DREJ) To remove sand or mud from a river or lake bottom so that large ships can pass without touching bottom.

Fingerling (FING ger ling) Small baby fish about the size of your finger.

Flail Farm tool used to thresh grain by hand. It has a handle on one end and a wooden piece that swings around on the other.

Fugitive (FYOU ji tive) Someone who is hiding out or trying to escape.

Garrison, garrisoned (GAR i sun) To place or station soldiers at a fort.

Geologist (ge OL o jist) A scientist who studies rocks and the way the earth is formed.

Girdle, girdled (GUR dul) To make a cut all the way around a tree through the outer bark and remove a ring of bark. This will kill the tree.

Glacial till (GLAY shul) Mud, clay, small stones, etc. left behind by a glacier when it melts.

Grants Gifts of land.

Grindstone Type of sandstone used to sharpen knives, axes, etc., or to grind and shape metal.

Grist Grains used to make flour.

Harbor, harbored To hide someone from the police, etc.

Harrow (HARE oh) Farm tool with long teeth or metal disks used to break up the soil for planting.

Hewn (HYOUN) Shaped with an axe or other special tool; wood is hewn.

Humus (HYOU mus) Dark, rich dirt formed from decaying leaves and plant material.

Huronia (hyou ROWN ee ah) The land of the Huron Indians in Ontario, Canada.

Huronian A time in the Precambrian period.

Husk, husking. To take the husk or outer covering off an ear of corn.

Interurban (in ter UR ban) Short railway line going between suburbs and downtown or between two nearby cities.

Jay's Treaty The treaty made by John Jay with the British in 1796 to turn over the Northwest Territory (including Michigan) to the United States.

Keel The very bottom of a boat; the long wooden beam at the bottom to which the ribs of a boat are attached.

Keweenawan (key win AW an) A geological time in the Precambrian period.

Locks A series of swinging doors in a canal used to hold water so that boats can be raised or lowered.

Longitude (LAWN ji tood) Imaginary lines going north and south around the world. Traveling east or west, you would pass various lines of longitude.

Loom A machine or frame for weaving cloth.

Macadam (mack AD am) Kind of paving material made of tar and gravel.

Meridian (me RID ee an) Imaginary lines going north and south around the world. Similar to lines of longitude.

Mississippian (miss iss IP ee an) Period when huge swamps developed with lots of plant life. These plants died and became the coal we mine today.

Moraine (mo RAYN) Hill or deposit of dirt and rocks left behind by a glacier.

Motherlode Main part of a large deposit of a mineral such as gold, copper, iron, silver, etc.

Mulatto (myou LAHT toh) Someone who has both black and white ancestors.

Nursery, tree Farm or greenhouse where plants are grown from seed for transplanting while they are still small.

Ordinance (OR di nans) A law; set of rules or regulations.

Ordovician (or do VISH ee an) Geological period when the sea began to develop higher forms of life such as jellyfish. Most of North America was under water then.

Palisades (pal i SAYDS) Strong fence made of tall wooden stakes stood on end and sharpened at the top.

Peninsula (pen IN su lah) A piece of land surrounded by water on three sides.

Pennsylvanian (pen sil VAYN yan) Geological period similar to the Mississippian when there were large swamps, big insects, and reptiles. Several mountain ranges were formed then.

Porous (POUR us) Something is porous which will let water soak through it. Cloth is porous, but glass is not.

Precambrian (pre KAM bree an) Geological time period when the basic formation of the earth occurred. There are few clues to life at this time.

Proportional representation This means that each member of congress represents the same number of people, not the same size area. Without this, people in rural areas often have more political power than people in cities.

Quarry, quarried (KWOR ee) To remove rock or stone from a type of open pit mine.

Quebec (kwe BEK or kay BEK) Mainly French-speaking province in Canada. Also the name of the province's capital city, which is on the St. Lawrence River.

Ranger Kind of soldier who usually ranges over an area to protect it.

Refine, refining (re FINE) To make a material-- usually a metal-- more pure by melting it and pouring off impurities.

Reservations (rez er VAY shuns) Land set aside for a special purpose, such as an Indian reservation. These supposedly belong to the Indians, but are controlled by the federal government too.

Rollway Place beside a river where logs were piled in winter so that in spring they could be rolled into the river and floated to a sawmill.

Sault Sainte Marie (Soo SAYNT ma REE) Sault is a French word for rapids or waterfall. This town is near a rapids and was named for Saint Marie by French missionaries.

Scale To estimate amount of board feet of lumber in a tree, an acre of woods, etc.

Scythe (SIGHTH-- pronounce the "th" as in "than") Tool with a large curved blade and long wooden handle used to cut grain or grass. It is held with both hands and swung from side to side.

Sedimentary (sed i MEN ta ree) Rock formed from a sediment like mud, clay or silt by heat and pressure.

Seed drills Farm machines used to plant seeds mechanically.

Shale A rock made by compressing mud or clay mixtures.

Sharp shod Shod means to wear shoes, as a horse does. The horse has more traction when his shoes have sharpened metal wedges on them--then he is "sharp shod".

Sheaves Bundles made of wheat or oat stalks tied together. They usually are stood upright in the field.

Shipwright (SHIP RITE) A person skilled in building ships.

Shocks Several sheaves of grain or corn stood together in the field, with a couple more covering the top of the pile. A way to store grain before it is threshed.

Sickle (SICK el) Hand tool used for cutting grain. It has a small C-shaped curved blade and is held in one hand.

Silurian (si LU ree an) Geological period after the Ordovician. By this time some forms of life were living on land.

Skip Small open railroad car usually used in mining. Sometimes it is a kind of large bucket used to raise or lower men and ore in a mine.

Smelt To melt ore or metal. (It is also a small silvery fish about five inches long.)

Spur Railroad branch off the main line.

Survey (sir VAY) To make careful measurements of land area; to locate boundary lines, etc.

Sweep A long pole to which horses were hitched. The horses walked in a circle, turning this pole or lever and giving power to a machine.

Taconite (TAK uh nite) Flint-like rock containing particles of iron oxide.

Territory (TAIR i tore ee) A large section of land that has some political organization, but is not yet a state of the United States; however, it is still a part of the country. Other countries can have territories as well.

Thames (TEMZ) A major river in England. It is also the name of rivers in Ontario and Connecticutt.

Thresh To strike grain with a flail or run it through a machine to separate the kernel from the rest of the plant.

Trace elements Chemicals that are needed by living things to grow, but needed only in very small amounts.

Trunk lines A system for long-distance travel; the main route of a highway, railroad, or airline.

Weathering agents Physical forces (rain, wind, snow, sand, heat, etc.) which wear down things that are outside.

Wheelwright (WHEEL RITE) A person who made wooden wheels for wagons before modern tires were invented.

Winnow, winnowed (WIN no) To separate grain by throwing it into the air and letting the husks, pieces of leaves, stems, and waste blow away.

Writ of Habeus Corpus (rit of HAY be us COR pus) This Latin phrase means "you have the body". It is a legal document which is very important in American law. It helps make sure that people are not jailed unless there is actual evidence that they have committed a crime. When someone asks the court for a writ of habeus corpus, the police must give the court the reasons a person is in jail. If the reasons are not legal or if there is not enough evidence, the person must be set free.

INDEX